GCE Applied Business:

External Influences
on the Business Enterprise

☐ Eddie McKee

cea
ewarding Learning

Colourpoint
Educational

© Eddie McKee and Colourpoint Books
   2007

ISBN: 978 1 904242 73 4

First Edition

First Impression

Layout and design: Colourpoint Books

Printed by: ColourBooks Ltd

The source for the ONS material on pages 8, 61, 69, 73 and 76 is the National Statistics website (www.statistics.gov.uk). The source for the HM Treasury material on pages 74 and 75 is the HM Treasury website (www.hm-treasury.gov.uk). This material is reproduced under the terms of the Click-Use Licence.
Crown copyright material is reproduced with the permission of the Controller of HMSO and the Queen's Printer for Scotland.

Colourpoint Books

Colourpoint House
Jubilee Business Park
21 Jubilee Road
Newtownards
County Down
Northern Ireland
BT23 4YH

Tel: 028 9182 0505
Fax: 028 9182 1900
E-mail: info@colourpoint.co.uk
Web site: www.colourpoint.co.uk

Eddie McKee is coordinator of Applied Business at St Louise's Comprehensive College, Belfast. He is also an experienced examiner for GCE Economics and GCE Applied Business.

This book was edited by Ian Bickerstaff. Ian is an experienced examiner, having acted as an assistant examiner for GCE Economics, and currently acting as a principal examiner of both GCE Business Studies and GCE Applied Business. He is also a principal moderator of the Wider Key Skills. Ian has a combined Honours degree in Economics and Education and a Master's degree in Business Administration (MBA). Ian is employed as a university lecturer, teaching Accounting, Strategic Issues and Entrepreneurship. He is currently researching Entrepreneurship Education. He is also the author of another book in this series entitled *GCE Applied Business: Finance*.

This book was endorsed by CCEA 07 June 2007.

Thanks must go to a number of people without whose help this book would not have been completed.

Firstly to my wife Natasha for her unending patience and support, to Eamon McCann for his priceless ability to recover work which had accidentally been erased or deleted, and to Amanda Swann at CCEA and Julie Trouton at Colourpoint for their words of advice and encouragement.

Go raibh míle maith agaibh.

For Caolán McAllister:

Imithe ar shíl na fírrine ach ní dhéanfaidh muid dearmad ort.

Picture credits:

Cover image: Harrison Photography, www.harrisonphotography.co.uk
Derek Polley: 4, 30
IStockphoto*: 5, 6, 10, 12, 14, 16, 21, 23, 37, 39, 40, 48, 50, 52, 53 (bottom), 54 (top), 58, 59, 60, 62, 66, 72, 78, 79, 86, 87, 89, 91, 96 (bottom)
FG Wilson: 8 (top)
Malcolm Johnston: 8 (bottom), 25, 32, 33, 54 (bottom), 93, 99
Sheila Johnston: 9, 26, 31, 35, 36, 42 (both top), 46, 49, 53 (top), 56, 81
Wesley Johnston: 29, 42 (both bottom), 67, 84
John Lewis: 45 (top)
Slieve Russell Hotel, Golf and Country Club: 47
Getty Images: 96 (top)

* Please see alongside individual images for photographers' member names.

CONTENTS

This text covers AS Unit 3 (External Influences on the Business Enterprise) of the CCEA Specification for GCE Applied Business.

LIST OF ABBREVIATIONS

CEO – chief executive officer

CPI – Consumer Price Index

DETINI – Department of Enterprise, Trade and Investment

DTI – Department of Trade and Industry

EMU – Economic and Monetary Union

Forex – foreign exchange

GDP – Gross Domestic Product

GNP – Gross National Product

ILO – International Labour Organization

JSA – Jobseeker's Allowance

MPC – Monetary Policy Committee

OFT – Office of Fair Trading

ONS – Office for National Statistics

PED – price elasticity of demand

PES – price elasticity of supply

SME – small or medium-sized enterprise

VAT – value-added tax

WTO – World Trade Organization

CHAPTER 1

Markets and industrial sectors

What is a business?

A **business** is typically defined as "any activity carried out by one or more people with the intention of producing goods or services that can then be sold on to others".

The aim of most businesses (although not all) is to carry out this production in such a way as to maximise the return for the owners of the business.

There are many different types of businesses operating in Northern Ireland which produce goods and services to sell in a variety of different markets.

What is a market?

A **market** is any place where buyers and sellers come together to exchange goods and services.

There are millions of markets all over the world, selling everything from oil to computers to financial assets like **bonds** and **shares**. There is even a market for footballers!

Traditionally a market was a physical space where **producers** and **consumers** came together to engage in trade. Many of the larger towns in Northern Ireland developed because they had a popular market. These towns are still often referred to as market towns, for example Cookstown in County Tyrone and Draperstown in County Derry. Within Belfast, some of the most famous areas are named after the market which took place there, such as Cornmarket in the heart of Belfast city centre.

Today, however, many markets involve trade which does not take place in a particular physical space. The term 'market' is simply used metaphorically to describe the trade which occurs in that industry.

With advances in technology and the development of **ecommerce**, producers and consumers no longer have to meet to engage in trade. The internet auction site eBay illustrates just how successful a **virtual market** can be.

Types of market

The Cornmarket, Belfast city centre

Markets can be classified under a number of different headings.

☐ COMMODITY MARKET

This is a market which involves trade in **raw materials** which will later be transformed into finished products.

Commodities include industrial metals such as copper and tin, precious metals such as gold and silver, raw food products such as coffee beans, sugar and wheat, as well as oil and other raw materials.

Commodities are traded in specialised markets called **exchanges**. For example, the London Metal Exchange (LME) is the arena for the trading of industrial metals such as copper, lead and zinc.

As the price of commodities is often volatile, special contracts known as **futures** are used when purchasing commodities. A futures contract is simply an agreement to purchase or sell a fixed quantity of a commodity at a future date at a prearranged price.

Purchasing commodities in this way allows a firm to plan for the future without having to worry about large changes to the price of its raw materials.

CONSUMER MARKET

This is a market for finished consumer goods which are purchased by the end consumer.

Consumer goods include items such as a jar of coffee, a loaf of bread, or a kilogram of cheese (often referred to as **consumables** or **non-durable goods**), and products such as cars, televisions, and computers (generally referred to as **consumer durables**).

The consumer market also includes trade in **intangibles** – products which cannot be seen and touched. These include services like personal banking, insurance and hairdressing.

CAPITAL GOODS MARKET

This is a market which involves the trade of **capital goods**.

Capital goods are those which can be used in the production of other products but are not incorporated into them – they are not a part of the final product. This includes things like equipment, machinery and tools.

These capital goods are purchased by firms to assist them in the production of other goods.

INDUSTRIAL MARKET

This is a market for goods which are used by industry but don't fall under the capital goods section. Examples of items which are traded in an industrial market include sand and gravel.

SPECIALIST MARKETS

The stock market

This is the market for the trading of financial assets such as company shares, bonds and other financial securities. These financial assets are listed and traded on what are known as **stock exchanges**.

A stock exchange is simply a mechanism which brings together the buyers and sellers of financial assets. In the United Kingdom (UK) the stock market is located in London and is known as the London Stock Exchange (LSE). The LSE is itself a company and since 2001 shares in LSE have been traded on the main LSE market.

The foreign exchange (forex) market

This is the market for the buying and selling of foreign currency. The main traders on the forex markets are large banks, central banks, currency speculators, multinational corporations (MNCs) and governments.

This is by far the world's largest market in terms of the value of trade, with over £400 billion being traded every day on the London forex market.

ACTIVITY 1.1

Using the internet, identify in which markets the following companies operate.

1. Nestlé	3. Caterpillar	5. Montupet	7. Toni & Guy
2. The Body Shop	4. HSBC	6. Audi	8. Readymix

Factors of production

A business will normally employ a variety of resources when it produces goods or services. These resources are usually divided into categories and are known as the factors of production.

☐ LAND

This refers not only to the actual physical land itself, but also to the minerals, raw materials, vegetation and wildlife that can be extracted from it. Some countries, for example Saudi Arabia, are naturally endowed with large quantities of natural resources such as oil, and their wealth depends on their ability to extract and exploit these resources.

☐ LABOUR

This refers to the workers who make the products. It includes the people who work directly in the production process and also those who are indirectly involved, for example clerical workers, support staff and management. Firms generally refer to their workers as their employees.

©iStockphoto.com/leezsnow

☐ CAPITAL

The term 'capital' has many meanings and is sometimes used to refer to the finance needed to start up and run the business. However, strictly speaking capital refers to:

- **Fixed capital** – the machinery and equipment used by the firm to produce its output
- **Working/circulating capital** – the stock of finished and semi-finished goods and components which will either be consumed in the future or used up in the production process

☐ ENTERPRISE

The term 'enterprise' or '**entrepreneurship**' refers to the management skills needed to bring all the other factors together, and make them work in a way that will produce a product or service which can then be sold to others at a profit.

An **entrepreneur** is therefore a risk-taker who brings the factors of production together – someone who has the skills to organise these factors and produce a good or service at a profit.

ACTIVITY 1.2

Famous entrepreneurs include Richard Branson (pictured right), Anita Roddick and Bill Gates.

Find out in what businesses these people are involved.

THE COST OF FACTORS OF PRODUCTION

A commonly-used statement in business is "There is no such thing as a free lunch." Employing factors of production will lead to the firm incurring costs, and these costs are normally classified as shown below:

Factor	Factor cost
Labour	Wages
Land	Rent
Capital	Interest (paid on the money borrowed to buy capital)
Enterprise	Profit

The structure of industry

The typical economy is made up of different sectors. These can be defined in various ways but the most common method of classification is to define the activity as either **primary**, **secondary**, **tertiary** or **quaternary**.

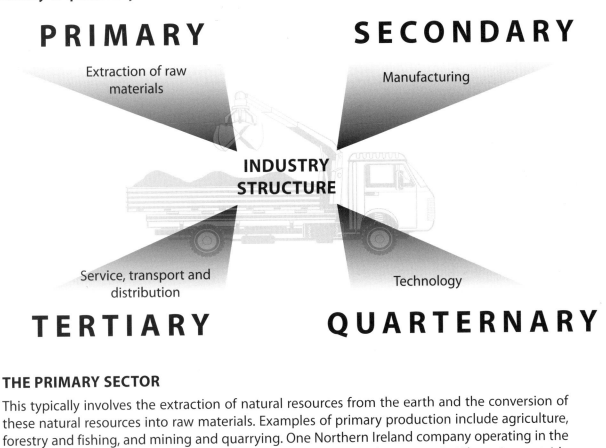

PRIMARY
Extraction of raw materials

SECONDARY
Manufacturing

INDUSTRY STRUCTURE

TERTIARY
Service, transport and distribution

QUARTERNARY
Technology

THE PRIMARY SECTOR

This typically involves the extraction of natural resources from the earth and the conversion of these natural resources into raw materials. Examples of primary production include agriculture, forestry and fishing, and mining and quarrying. One Northern Ireland company operating in the primary sector is Irish Salt Mining & Exploration Company, which operates in Kilroot, just outside Carrickfergus.

THE SECONDARY SECTOR

This usually involves taking the raw materials produced by the primary sector and converting them into finished or semi-finished goods to be sold to the final consumer or to other businesses. Examples of secondary activity include the manufacture of clothing and electronics, and construction. One Northern Ireland company which operates in the secondary sector is FG Wilson, which has bases in Belfast and Larne and is one of the world's largest manufacturers of electricity generators.

THE TERTIARY SECTOR

This is often referred to as the **service sector** of the economy and typically includes the provision of services to business and the final consumer. Examples of tertiary sector activity include transport and distribution, insurance and banking, and leisure and tourism. One Northern Ireland company operating in the tertiary sector is Translink, which operates Ulsterbus, Citybus and Northern Ireland Railways (NIR).

FG Wilson's base in Larne

THE QUATERNARY SECTOR

Some people now refer to a fourth sector of the economy as the quaternary sector. This sector involves intellectual services such as research and development, and information management. However, many economists regard the quaternary sector as simply a subsection of the tertiary sector, and it is still treated this way in official government classifications.

Examples of quaternary activity include education, consulting, and information and communication technology. One company which operates in the quaternary sector in Northern Ireland is PricewaterhouseCoopers, which provides tax advisory and consultancy services to both public and private enterprises.

PricewaterhouseCoopers' Belfast base

ACTIVITY 1.3

The table below shows the percentage of the labour force employed in the three main industrial sectors in the UK between 1985 and 2006.

Industrial sector	1985	1995	2006
Primary	7	4	3
Secondary	37	32	19
Tertiary	56	64	78

Source: ONS

Using the information in the table:

1. Draw a chart showing the trends in industrial sector employment from 1985 to 2006.
2. Describe the trends as shown in the chart.
3. Explain why you think these trends may be occurring.

☐ OVERLAP BETWEEN SECTORS

There is considerable overlap between each of these sectors. We have already noted that for many economists the quaternary sector is simply a subsection of the tertiary sector. In addition, in official classification the packaging and processing of raw materials which takes place close to the primary producers is often considered to constitute primary activity – even though processing and packaging would normally be thought of as secondary activity. This is especially true if the raw materials require some processing before they can be sold on to manufacturers.

Trying to classify a firm as operating mainly in the primary, secondary or tertiary sectors is also very difficult since many firms operate across more than one sector. A firm is described as being **fully vertically integrated** if it operates across all three sectors. For example, some food retailers which operate in the tertiary sector have their own farms which grow the food (which constitutes primary activity), and their own food-processing plants to process the food (which constitutes secondary activity).

The chain of production

The chain of production is the term used to describe the various stages involved in the production of a particular product.

To illustrate this, consider the processes involved in the production of a chocolate bar. Like most goods, a chocolate bar begins in the primary sector with the growing and harvesting of cocoa beans. Cocoa beans are grown mainly in South America, West Africa and more recently Southeast Asia, with over 40% of the world's supply coming from the Ivory Coast.

The next stage in the chain of production is the manufacturing process. In this stage large chocolate producers such as Nestlé, Cadbury and Mars take the cocoa beans and other raw materials such as sugar and milk and convert them into chocolate bars and sweets.

The final stage in the chain is the tertiary stage where the chocolate products are sold to us – the final consumer – through retail outlets such as shops and restaurants.

REVISION QUESTIONS

1. Explain what is meant by the term 'market'.
2. What goods or services are sold in the following markets?
   (a) Stock market   (b) Forex market
3. Identify the market in which the following goods would be sold:
   (a) Aluminium   (c) Televisions   (e) Raw coffee beans   (g) Network of computers
   (b) Tractors   (d) Sand   (f) Banking
4. Explain, using an example, the term 'consumer durable'.
5. What are the four factors of production and what are the costs associated with employing these factors?
6. Using examples, explain how a car could be classified as both a consumer good and a capital good.
7. Using two examples in each case distinguish between the primary, secondary and tertiary sectors of industry.
8. Give two reasons why the number of people employed in the secondary sector in the UK has fallen in recent years.

CHAPTER 2

The theory of demand and supply

In the previous chapter we learned that a market is a place where buyers and sellers come together to exchange goods and services. In this exchange, buyers *demand* goods from the market and sellers *supply* goods to the market.

The theory of demand and supply is therefore an attempt to explain how the *price* of these goods and services would be determined in a competitive market.

Demand

The theory of demand deals with how consumers behave when they are faced with a change in the price of a good – if this changes, will consumers be likely to purchase more of the product or less of the product?

Economists define demand as "the quantity of a good or service that a consumer is willing and able to buy at a given price in a given time period". The phrase "willing and able" is very important, as it is only when a consumer is both *willing* to purchase a product and *able* to purchase it that the demand becomes effective. For example, I may be very *willing* to purchase a new BMW, but if I don't have the funds to support this desire then I am not *able* to go to the market and demand the car.

☐ HOW DOES THE QUANTITY DEMANDED OF A GOOD CHANGE WHEN PRICE CHANGES?

For most goods we would expect the quantity demanded to *increase* when price *decreases*. For example, if the price of a new BMW fell from £30,000 to £10,000 I may well be able to back up my desire to purchase the car with the funds to do so, and therefore the quantity demanded of BMWs would increase.

©iStockphoto.com/Marlee90

Therefore, we can say that there is an *inverse relationship* between the price of a good and the quantity demanded of that good.

If we were to plot the price of a good on a vertical axis and the quantity demanded on a horizontal axis, we could show this relationship as a graph or diagram. The **demand curve** for a good or service would slope downwards from left to right. As price increases people will buy less of the good, and vice versa.

This is shown on the diagram below.

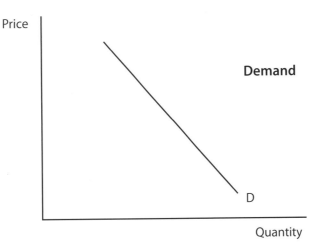

ACTIVITY 2.1

The table below shows the estimated daily sales of a local newspaper at five different prices.

Price	Daily sales (est)
55p	191,000
50p	234,000
45p	295,000
40p	325,000
30p	350,000

1. Using the information in the table above, plot a daily demand curve for this paper.
2. Using the graph, estimate the likely daily sales if the selling price was:
   (a) 35p
   (b) 48p
3. Calculate the sales revenue the publisher would be likely to receive if it sold the paper at 50p.

Supply

The theory of supply deals with how producers behave when they are faced with a change in the price of a good – if this changes will producers be likely to supply more of the product or less of the product?

Economists define supply as "the quantity of a good or service that producers are willing and able to supply onto a market at a given price in a given time period".

HOW DOES THE QUANTITY SUPPLIED CHANGE WHEN PRICE OF A GOOD CHANGES?

For most goods we would expect quantity supplied to *increase* when price *increases*. As the price of a particular good increases, producers will shift resources to the production of that good as it represents a better return on their investment – therefore, the quantity of the good supplied will increase.

Therefore, we can say that there is a *positive relationship* between the price of a good or service and quantity supplied of that good or service.

If we were to plot the price of a good on a vertical axis and the quantity supplied on a horizontal axis, we could show this relationship as a graph or diagram. The **supply curve** for a good or service would slope upwards from left to right. As price increases the quantity that firms are willing to supply onto the market increases, and vice versa.

This is shown on the diagram below.

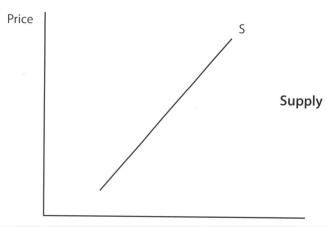

ACTIVITY 2.2

The table below shows the quantity of a local newspaper that the publisher would be willing to supply at five different prices.

Price	Daily production
55p	375,000
50p	334,000
45p	295,000
40p	225,000
30p	190,000

1. Using the information in the table above plot a daily supply curve for the local newspaper.
2. Using the graph estimate the likely daily print-run if the selling price was:
   (a) 35p   (b) 48p

How is the price of a good or service determined?

The price at which the good or service is sold is determined by the interaction of demand for the good or service and the supply of the good or service. The process through which the forces of demand and supply interact to determine price is known as the **market (or price) mechanism**. When buyers and sellers come together they create a market where demand and supply interact to determine what economists call the **market clearing** or **equilibrium price**.

This is the price where quantity demanded is equal to quantity supplied, as illustrated by the demand and supply cross diagram below.

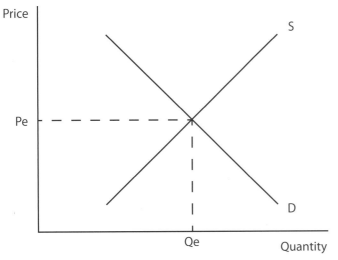

Pe = equilibrium price

Qe = equilibrium quantity
(demanded and supplied)

At price Pe the amount producers are willing to supply Qe is exactly equal to the amount consumers are willing to buy Qe, and therefore there is no tendency for the price to change.

DISEQUILIBRIUM

Disequilibrium occurs when there is a situation of **excess demand** – where quantity demanded is greater than the quantity supplied.

It also occurs when there is a situation of **excess supply** – where quantity supplied is greater than the quantity demanded.

Excess demand

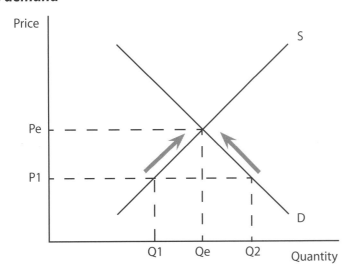

If a firm sets its price at P1 then the quantity that consumers are willing and able to buy would equal Q2, which is greater than the amount that producers are willing and able to supply (Q1).

Therefore, there is a shortage of the good. When this occurs, the price of the good would then be **bid up** until the equilibrium price is restored.

Excess supply

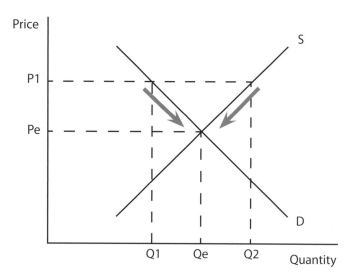

If a firm sets its price at P1 then the amount that producers are willing and able to supply increases to Q2, but the amount that consumers are willing and able to buy falls to Q1.

We therefore have excess supply. In order to sell this excess supply the producer must decrease price until the equilibrium price is restored.

ACTIVITY 2.3

Using the information provided in Activity 2.1 and 2.2:

1. Plot a demand and supply cross diagram and use it to estimate the equilibrium price for the local newspaper.
2. Explain what would happen in the market if the publisher sets a price of:
   (a) 30p
   (b) 55p

The conditions of demand

We have already seen how a change in the price of a good will cause a change in the quantity demanded of that good. As price increases quantity demanded will fall and vice versa.

However, demand also depends on many factors other than price. These other factors are known as the conditions of demand.

A change in any one of the conditions of demand will cause the demand curve to shift. If the demand curve shifts to the right this represents an *increase* in demand, and if it shifts to the left this represents a *decrease* in demand.

©iStockphoto.com/vpopovic

INCOME

This is a very important factor in determining the level of demand for a particular product or service.

For most goods, or what economists call **normal goods**, demand will increase as income increases. Consider the example of new cars. An increase in incomes will increase the demand for new cars and the demand curve will shift to the right as shown below. Therefore, more new cars will be demanded at every price level.

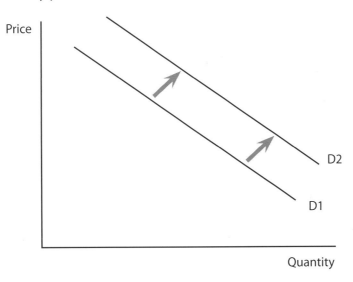

However, for some goods, or what economists call **inferior goods**, demand will fall when income rises. Consider the market for second-hand clothes. As incomes increase the demand for second-hand clothes will fall and the demand curve will shift to the left.

THE PRICE OF RELATED GOODS

Another important factor in determining the level of demand for a good or service is the price of other closely related goods and services.

Complements

Sometimes two goods are demanded jointly, for example camera and film. Economists refer to these goods as **complements**. When the price of one of these goods increases the demand for the other will fall.

Substitutes

Sometimes goods are in competitive demand and can be used as substitutes for each other, for example Ariel and Persil. When the price of one of these goods increases the demand for the other is also likely to increase. For example, an increase in the price of Persil will lead to an increase in the demand for Ariel as Ariel now represents greater value for money relative to Persil.

TASTES AND FASHIONS

Changes in tastes and fashions can have a huge impact on the demand for certain goods and services. When products become fashionable demand will increase, but demand will fall if tastes change and the good becomes unfashionable. For example, the demand for flares fluctuated greatly as tastes and fashions changed.

☐ ADVERTISING

An effective advertising campaign can cause demand for a product to increase at every price level. This explains why firms spend such huge amounts of money advertising and marketing their products. For more information on advertising, see page 54.

☐ GOVERNMENT POLICY

Government policy is another important factor which influences the demand for a good or service. Changes to legislation can have huge effects on the demand for a good. Consider the impact of the introduction of the smoking ban in public places on the market for cigarettes.

Changes to income tax and interest rates will also impact upon the demand for certain products. For example, if the Monetary Policy Committee (MPC) cuts interest rates, the demand for housing and other goods bought on credit would be likely to increase.

☐ POPULATION

As the population increases the demand for most goods would increase. In addition, changes to the structure of the population can affect demand. For example an increase in the birth rate would lead to an increase in the demand for baby clothes.

☐ EXPECTED PRICE CHANGES OR CHANGES IN EXPECTATIONS ABOUT FUTURE EVENTS

If people believe that the price of a good, for example oil, is going to increase in the future they will increase their demand today, and vice versa. If you believe that the new coat you want is going to be cheaper tomorrow when the sales start you may well wait till then to purchase the coat.

Similarly, businesses which use large quantities of a particular raw material may stockpile that raw material if they are worried that there might be a shortage in the future.

Shifts of the demand curve

A change in any one of the conditions of demand will cause the demand curve to shift and will lead to a new equilibrium price and quantity. The diagram below shows an increase in demand.

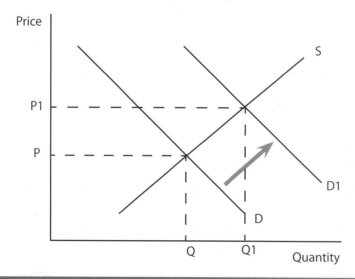

You can see that the increase in demand has shifted the demand curve to the right, and has led to an increase in price and quantity demanded and supplied. The increase in demand has caused an extension of supply – an increase in quantity supplied.

Similarly, a fall in demand will lead to a fall in the equilibrium price and a fall in quantity demanded and supplied.

ACTIVITY 2.4

Explain, with the aid of a diagram, how the market would be affected in the following situations.

1. A rise in the demand for potato bread on the market for potatoes
2. A rise in train fares on bus and taxi services
3. A fall in interest rates on the market for housing
4. A fall in the price of tea on the market for coffee
5. A rise in the price of computers on the market for computers

The conditions of supply

We have already seen how a change in the price of a good will cause a change in the quantity supplied of that good – there will be a movement along the supply curve.

However, just like demand, supply also depends on factors other than price. These are known as the conditions of supply. A change in one of these conditions will cause the supply curve to shift as shown below.

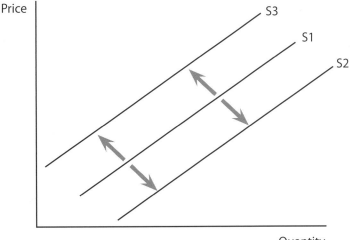

An increase in supply will shift the supply curve to the right from S1 to S2. A decrease in supply, on the other hand, will shift the supply curve to the left from S1 to S3.

Anything which increases the cost of production will reduce supply and therefore shift the supply curve to the left (S1 to S3).

Anything which decreases the cost of production will increase supply and shift the supply curve to the right (S1 to S2).

☐ PRICE OF FACTORS OF PRODUCTION

One factor influencing the supply of a product is the price of the factors of production used in making that product. For example, an increase in the cost of raw materials or wages will cause the firm's costs to increase and will in turn cause the supply curve to shift to the left. In other words, an increase in the cost of raw materials and wages will cause a reduction in the supply.

☐ PRODUCTIVITY OF FACTORS OF PRODUCTION

Changes in productivity rates will also have an influence on supply. If the firm is able to increase labour productivity it will shift the supply curve to the right. Similarly, a reduction in productivity rates, for example caused by industrial action on the behalf of employees, will reduce productivity and therefore the supply curve will shift to the left.

☐ INDIRECT TAXES AND SUBSIDIES

Changes in government policy impact upon supply as well as demand. For example, if the government places an indirect tax like value-added tax (VAT) on a product it will shift the supply curve to the left. A subsidy, on the other hand, will reduce the cost of producing the good and will therefore shift the supply curve to the right.

☐ TECHNOLOGICAL ADVANCES

Changes in the level of technology will also have an impact on the ability of a firm to supply goods onto a market. Technological advances such as the development of the internet and ecommerce will reduce the costs of supplying a good and therefore shift the supply curve to the right.

☐ NATURAL FACTORS

The weather can play a very important role in the production of agricultural products in particular. For example, bad weather conditions and the resulting poor crops can cause the supply curve to shift to the left, which in turn will cause an increase in the price of the product.

Shifts of the supply curve

A change in any one of the conditions of supply will cause the supply curve to shift and will lead to a new equilibrium price and quantity. The diagram below shows an increase in supply.

As you can see, an increase in supply will shift the supply curve to the right and lead to a reduction in the equilibrium price and an increase in the equilibrium quantity demanded and supplied.

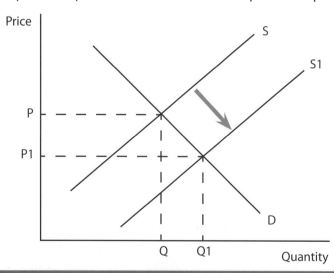

Similarly, a fall in supply will shift the supply curve to the left and lead to an increase in the equilibrium price and a reduction in the equilibrium quantity demanded and supplied.

ACTIVITY 2.5

Explain, with the aid of a diagram, how the market would be affected in the following situations.

1. A rise in the cost of steel on the market for new cars
2. An increase in subsidy given to Translink on the cost of train fares
3. A fall in the cost of timber on the market for new houses
4. A fall in the price of chocolate on the market for chocolate
5. An increase in VAT on the market for MP3 players

Changes to demand or supply

When economists talk about an increase in demand or supply they mean that the demand curve or supply curve has shifted. If they talk about an increase in quantity demanded or supplied they mean there has been a movement along the demand or supply curve.

In the diagram opposite there has been an increase in supply (the supply curve has shifted), and this has led to an increase in quantity demanded (a movement along the demand curve).

When explaining a diagram or a change in market conditions, be careful not to confuse changes in demand with changes in quantity demanded, or changes in supply with changes in quantity supplied. They are very different things.

ACTIVITY 2.6

Using a diagram, explain how the following would affect the market for sugar.

1. Bad weather conditions
2. A fall in the price of fertiliser and sugar being seen as unhealthy
3. An increase in farm-workers' wages and an increase in income tax paid by consumers
4. A reduction in the subsidies paid to farmers through the Common Agricultural Policy

Elasticity

We have seen that changes in price will cause changes in both quantity demanded and quantity supplied. For example, when price increases we know that quantity demanded will fall and quantity supplied will increase.

However, firms are also keen to know exactly how much quantity demanded or supplied would change if price changed. They can discover this information through using the concept of elasticity.

In an economic context, elasticity means **responsiveness** – it measures the responsiveness of one economic variable to a change in some other variable.

We will study two types of elasticity – **price elasticity of demand** and **price elasticity of supply**.

PRICE ELASTICITY OF DEMAND (PED)

PED measures how responsive quantity demanded is to a change in price. In other words, it tells us how important price is in determining whether or not consumers buy a product.

If demand is sensitive to price (when price increases, quantity demanded decreases by a large amount) then the good is said to be price **elastic**. If demand is not sensitive to price changes then the good is said to be price **inelastic**.

PED is measured by using the following formula:

$$\frac{\% \text{ change in quantity demanded}}{\% \text{ change in price}}$$

For example, if price increased from £20 to £25 and demand fell from 100 to 90 as a result, then the PED would be calculated as follows:

% change in quantity demanded = 10/100 multiplied by 100 = 10%

% change in price = 5/20 multiplied by 100 = 25%

PED = 10%/25% = **0.4**

Strictly speaking the answer should be –0.4 as quantity demanded fell as price rose. However, it is acceptable to omit the minus sign when calculating PED as the figure will always be negative.

Relatively inelastic

When demand is relatively inelastic it takes a large percentage change in price to cause a relatively small percentage change in quantity demanded. The numerical value will be between zero and one and the demand curve will slope steeply, as shown below.

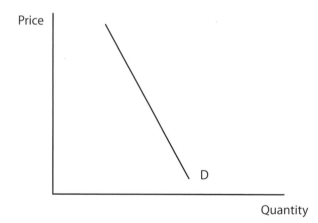

Relatively inelastic goods are normally addictive or have few substitutes, for example cigarettes. Therefore, when price increases consumers continue to purchase these products.

Relatively elastic

In this case a small percentage change in price will lead to a relatively large percentage change in quantity demanded. The numerical value will be greater than one, and the demand curve will be relatively flat, as shown opposite.

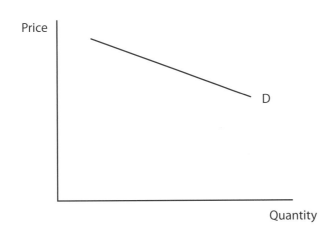

©iStockphoto.com/jsmith

Relatively elastic goods normally have a large number of substitutes, so when price increases consumers switch to the consumption of the substitute good.

What determines the elasticity of demand?

Necessity – if a good is a necessity then people will continue to buy it even when price increases, and therefore demand will be price inelastic, for example electricity.

Addiction – if goods are addictive or habit-forming then a large change in price will cause a very small change in quantity demanded, and therefore the demand for goods will be price inelastic, for example alcohol and drugs.

Availability of substitutes – the greater the number of substitutes there are for a good the more responsive demand will be to a change in price. Demand will therefore be price elastic. For example, the demand for package holidays is likely to be price elastic since there are a wide range of alternative package holidays on offer.

Percentage of income spent on the good – if you spend a low percentage of your income on a good then you are unlikely to notice a large percentage change in price. For example, if a box of matches increases in price from 5p to 10p it will have very little impact on sales, even though price has increased by 100%.

Time – demand tends to be more elastic over a long period. For example, if oil prices increase people who have oil central heating will still buy oil in the short term, as they need it, and therefore demand is inelastic. However, if oil prices stay high then, over the longer term, they may decide to switch to gas, and so demand becomes more elastic.

Why do firms calculate PED?

If a firm is contemplating raising the price of its product it is useful to know whether this increase in price would lead to an increase or a decrease in total revenue.

If demand is price inelastic (where the value for PED is less than 1) then an increase in price will lead to a smaller percentage change in quantity demanded, and therefore total revenue will increase. For example, if PED = 0.5 then a 10% increase in price would lead to a 5% decrease in quantity demanded, and therefore total revenue would be higher after the price increase.

However, if demand is price elastic ((where the value for PED is more than 1) then an increase in price would lead to a larger percentage decrease in quantity demanded, and therefore total revenue would decrease. For example, if PED = 3 then a 10% increase in price would lead to a 30% decrease in quantity demanded, and therefore total revenue would be lower after the price increase. On the other hand, a 10% reduction in price would lead to a 30% increase in quantity demanded, leading to an increase in total revenue. In summary:

- If demand is price **in**elastic the firm should **in**crease price to **in**crease total revenue.
- If demand is price elastic the firm should decrease price to increase total revenue.

☐ PRICE ELASTICITY OF SUPPLY (PES)

PES measures how responsive quantity supplied is to a change in price. In other words, it tells us how much more of a good will be offered for sale if price rises.

PES is measured by using the following formula:

$$\frac{\text{\% change in quantity supplied}}{\text{\% change in price}}$$

For example, if price increased from £20 to £25 (25%) and quantity supplied increased from 100 to 110 (10%), then PES = 10%/25% = **0.4**

Unlike PED, the figure for PES will always be positive.

Relatively inelastic

In this case it requires a large percentage change in price to produce a much smaller percentage change in quantity supplied. The numerical value for PES will be less than one and the supply curve will be relatively steep, as shown below.

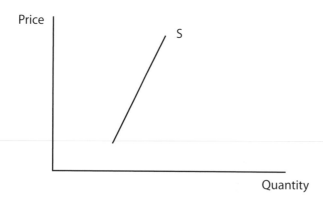

Relatively elastic

In this case a relatively small change in price will lead to a much larger change in quantity supplied. The numerical value will be greater than one and the supply curve will be relatively flat.

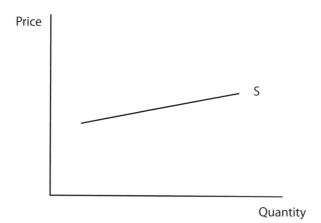

Perfectly inelastic

In this case the quantity supplied will not change no matter what happens to price. The numerical value will be zero and the supply curve will be a vertical line, as shown below.

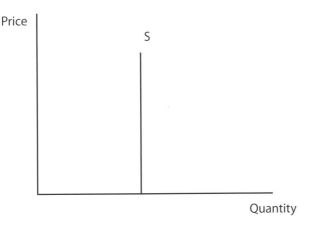

This type of elasticity is normally seen with sporting events or musical concerts where the venue can only hold a fixed number of people, regardless of what happens to price.

What determines the elasticity of supply?

The elasticity of supply depends upon the ease and speed with which supply can be changed in response to a change in market conditions.

Time – the distinguished economist Alfred Marshall pointed out that the longer the delay in measuring the change in supply following the change in price, the more elastic supply would be, since firms had more time to adjust their production plans.

For example, agricultural products tend to have relatively inelastic supply curves since it can take up to a year to increase supply when price increases. Some products like rubber can take up to five years to grow and therefore supply is very inelastic. On the other hand, manufactured goods tend to have more elastic supply curves since the production process is shorter.

The availability of stocks – if firms have stocks of finished goods available then they will be able to supply more of the good easily when demand or price increase, and therefore supply is regarded as being elastic.

The level of spare capacity in the industry – if an industry is operating at below full capacity and there are unemployed resources, then the industry will be able to increase supply easily. Therefore, supply will be more elastic. If, however, the industry is operating at full capacity, supply will be relatively inelastic.

©iStockphoto.com/vpopovic

☐ USING THE CONCEPTS OF ELASTICITY OF DEMAND AND SUPPLY

Firms will find it useful to have knowledge of both PED and PES. However, their usefulness should not be overstated and there are a number of potential problems with the values calculated.

Often the estimated values for PED and PES are calculated using past data. This is problematic, as just because a 10% fall in price brought about a 20% increase in quantity demanded in the past, does not mean that a further 10% decrease in price will bring about a further 20% increase in quantity demanded now. It must always be remembered that past performance can be a very poor indicator of future performance.

In addition, not all goods have a set price. Some goods, for example tea and sugar, are sold to consumers at different prices from different outlets, so when measuring PED how do we measure the change in price? Do we take an average price? If so, then this will surely effect the accuracy of the figure.

Finally, when calculating PED we use an assumption known as *ceteris paribus*, which means "all other things being equal". For example, if we calculate PED = 4 we make the claim that a 10% increase in price brought about a 40% decrease in quantity demanded. However, in reality the 40% decrease in quantity demanded may have occurred for reasons other than the increase in price, such as bad publicity about the product, a decrease in income of consumers, or a range of other factors.

For these reasons, using PED estimates to make predictions about what might happen in the future is fraught with difficulty.

Despite these problems, if used with caution and in conjunction with a range of other data, estimates of elasticity can prove very useful to firms.

Case Study: The Northern Ireland housing market

There has been a massive increase in house prices in Britain and Northern Ireland in recent years. Prices have grown on average by about 15% per year, and the average house price in Northern Ireland is now over £190,000.

This increase in the price of houses is a result of both **demand-side factors** and **supply-side factors**.

☐ DEMAND-SIDE FACTORS

- There has been an increase in the number of people of house-buying age.
- There has also been an increase in the divorce rate, resulting in families needing more than one house.
- There has been a significant increase in average incomes in Northern Ireland in recent years. This has led to a large increase in the demand for housing, since houses are an income elastic good.
- Societal changes have led to an increased independence of both the young and the old.
- There has been a significant fall in real interest rates from about 13% in 1990 to 5% in 2006. This affects the demand for housing, since houses are almost always bought with credit.
- The peace process has also led to an increase in demand for houses from speculators, particularly from the Republic of Ireland. Household incomes in the Republic of Ireland have increased substantially in recent years, and this has led to citizens of the Republic of Ireland looking for investment opportunities in Northern Ireland.

All of the above factors have shifted the demand curve for housing to the right.

At the same time, the supply of housing for sale has not increased by the same quantity. Housing supply is relatively inelastic, even in the long run, because of a lack of available building land and planning restrictions which limit the amount of houses that can be built. This is especially true in and around Belfast, which has experienced some of the largest increases in price.

The combination of these demand and supply-side factors has led to the huge increase in house prices, as illustrated opposite.

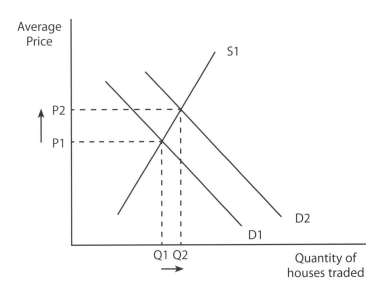

This diagram shows the effect of an increase in demand on the price of housing. Because the supply of housing is relatively inelastic, any increase in demand is likely to lead to a large increase in price.

REVISION QUESTIONS

1. On a diagram draw a demand curve and explain the relationship between price and quantity demanded.

2. On a diagram sketch a supply curve and explain the relationship between price and quantity supplied.

3. List the seven factors which would cause the demand curve to shift.

4. List the five factors which would cause the supply curve to shift.

5. Explain what is meant by the term 'inferior goods'.

6. Explain, with examples, the difference between 'substitutes' and 'complements'.

7. Explain how an increase in the rate of interest would impact upon the demand for:
   (a) cars
   (b) potatoes

8. Show on a diagram what would happen to the market for DVD players if the government:
   (a) increased the rate of VAT
   (b) decreased the rate of income tax

9. Explain why, for some goods, quantity demanded is relatively unresponsive to a change in the price of the good.

10. Explain why firms would want to calculate PED.

11. Explain why the supply of tickets to the All-Ireland Hurling Final could be described as being perfectly inelastic.

CASE STUDY

Cadbury wants to blitz Wrigley with a new gum called Trident (Adapted from the *Guardian*, 31 October 2006)

Cadbury Schweppes, the world's largest confectionery group, is to challenge the dominance of Wrigley in the UK chewing gum market with the launch next year of its American brand Trident.

The move, announced yesterday by Todd Stitzer, its chief executive, at an investor seminar, is part of Cadbury's wider efforts to focus its marketing activities on a smaller number of the group's stronger brands. The Cadbury's boss also told investors that the group, which is under pressure from rising production costs, was to abandon its long-standing targets for annual margin growth of between 0.5 and 0.75 of a percentage point.

Mr Stitzer also said that the group would adopt a dividend payment policy more in line with earnings. For the current year, the final dividend is likely to be increased by 10%, taking the total to 9.9p and leaving the annual rate of increase at 8%.

The British gum market has been shrinking over the last two years, but Wrigley, the dominant firm in the market with a 98% share, insists it is confident it can fend off a competitor such as Cadbury without having to resort to a price war. "We believe Cadbury will be a solid competitor, but we know how to hold on to our market position," said Gharry Eccles, UK managing director of Wrigley. The company is also market leader in the United States (US) market, where it sells twice as much gum as Cadbury brands.

Four years ago Cadbury had tried to take on Wrigley's dominance of the UK, its home market, with the launch of Trebor 24/7, a gum variant of the mint-flavoured sweet brand. The product flopped and was ditched within 18 months. Since then, however, Cadbury has acquired US gum specialist Adams, which brought with it the fast-growing Trident brand, the number two gum in the world behind Wrigley's Orbit. The Cadbury's gum stable also includes Dentyne, Bubblicious and Clorets.

Mr Stitzer noted the UK gum market had shrunk by 6% last year and 5% in 2004. "The British chewing gum market is going backwards and needs competition to drive the market," he said. Cadbury hopes its strong UK distribution network will help it mount a more serious challenge to Wrigley this time.

Simon Baldry, managing director of Cadbury Trebor Bassett (the UK arm of Cadbury Schweppes), said "We see massive potential in the UK for Trident. [It] is one of the top 10 gum markets in the world."

Last week Cadbury blamed the hot summer and product recalls for a weaker-than-expected confectionery market. Sales since the beginning of July fell by 5% compared with the same period in 2005.

Asked whether trends toward healthier eating were having an impact on sales, Mr Stitzer said "Despite obesity scares, the global confectionery market still grows at 4% to 5% a year, while less than 2% of a British person's diet is confectionery."

Using the information opposite, answer these questions.

1. Using a demand and supply diagram, explain what impact rising production costs are likely to have on the market for chewing gum.

2. Explain what is meant by the term 'dividend payment'.

3. Explain why producers like Wrigley produce more than one brand of chewing gum.

4. Explain how a hot summer could be blamed for weaker-than-expected confectionery sales.

5. Using demand and supply analysis, explain the impact concerns over obesity are likely to have on the UK confectionery market.

6. How might a company like Cadbury Schweppes react to this change in market conditions?

CHAPTER 3

The competitive environment

In the previous chapter we looked at how the demand for, and the supply of, a product interact to determine the equilibrium or market clearing price.

In this chapter we will examine how the structure of the market in which the firm operates influences the power the firm has to determine the price of its goods and services. The way in which a firm behaves, and the strategies it adopts to achieve its objectives, will very much depend upon the nature of the market in which it operates, and the level of competition it faces. Taking account of the nature of the market, and the level of competition faced by a firm, is very important whenever a producer is contemplating a change in price or indeed any change to its marketing mix.

Economists single out a number of key characteristics which will have a huge influence on the way individual firms behave. These characteristics determine the structure of the market and include:

- the number of firms in the industry and their relative size
- the extent to which the products produced by individual firms are similar
- the ease or difficulty with which new firms can enter or leave the industry (**barriers to entry**)
- the extent to which firms in the industry have the ability to earn **abnormal** or **supernormal** profits

The number and size of firms, and similarity of products

We are going to look at four different market structures which are outlined below. They are explored in more detail later in the chapter.

☐ PERFECTLY COMPETITIVE MARKET

This is characterised by a large number of small firms producing identical goods. There are no barriers to entry and abnormal profits can only be made in the short run.

☐ COMPETITIVE MARKET (MONOPOLISTIC COMPETITION)

This is characterised by a relatively large number of small firms producing similar (but not identical) products. There are no barriers to entry and abnormal profits can only be made in the short run.

☐ OLIGOPOLY

In an oligopoly there are several large firms selling similar products. There are some barriers to entry and abnormal profits can be made in the long run.

☐ MONOPOLY

A monopoly is when one large firm produces all the output in the industry. The term can also refer to the firm itself. Barriers to entry exist which prevent other firms entering the industry. Abnormal profits can be made in the long run.

Barriers to entry

One of the most important factors in determining the structure of a market, and therefore the conduct and behaviour of firms in that market, is the ease with which firms can enter or leave the industry.

If firms find it difficult to enter an industry, then we would say that barriers to entry exist. Barriers to entry are those characteristics of an industry that prevent potential competitors from entering it. They include the following.

☐ GOVERNMENT RESTRICTIONS

Firms sometimes find it very difficult to enter a particular industry as it is illegal to do so without a government **licence**. For example, a licence is required before a firm can engage in radio broadcasting or sell alcohol. This therefore acts as a barrier to entry. A **patent** is another example of a barrier to entry since it gives a firm the sole right to produce a product for a given period of time.

☐ ADVERTISING

In some industries firms spend huge amounts on advertising in an attempt to deter possible entrants. If new firms wish to compete with the more established firms they will have to spend similar amounts on advertising, but this level of spending is often beyond the means of small firms.

☐ SUNK COSTS

In certain circumstances it can be very difficult to leave an industry whenever things go wrong. If firms know that they will find it difficult to leave an industry should they experience difficult trading conditions, they may be reluctant to enter it in the first place. For example, in some industries large amounts of money will have to be invested which is not recoverable if things go wrong. These unrecoverable costs are known as sunk costs. Firms may be reluctant to enter an industry which requires these sunk costs.

Barriers to entry are the key factor in determining whether firms can earn abnormal profits in the long run. If barriers to entry exist in an industry then a firm will have the ability to earn long-run abnormal profits. If, however, there are no barriers to entry then the firm might be able to make abnormal profits in the short run, but will be unable to earn abnormal profits in the long run.

The ability to earn abnormal or supernormal profits

An abnormal or supernormal profit is defined by economists as "any profit over and above the minimum required to keep an entrepreneur producing in that industry". Abnormal profits are therefore those which exceed what an entrepreneur would normally be expected to earn through the employment of a similar combination of factors of production.

In 2005 the international banking corporation HSBC reported an operating profit of £11.5 billion, which represents a profit of approximately £22,000 per minute. In 2006 the oil exploration company Shell reported a second quarter profit of £3.7 billion, which is equivalent to approximately £28,000 per minute.

For many people these profits could be described as excessive. There were calls in the national press for government action to curb the abnormal profits of these companies, with some economists calling for a windfall tax on the profits of banks and oil companies.

However, both companies claimed that these huge profits were a result of sound business practice and were therefore not excessive. Indeed, the chief executive officer (CEO) of a major UK bank is reported to have stated that he "did not know what abnormal profits were and that no level of company profit could be described as excessive".

HOW DO WE DETERMINE IF PROFITS ARE NORMAL OR ABNORMAL?

To determine if abnormal profits are being earned by a firm, economists could compare the firm's profits with other firms in the same industry. However, if all firms in the industry are making abnormal profits then this comparison will reveal very little.

Another approach is to compare the firm's profits with those of similar-sized firms in other industries. The problem with this comparison is that it does not allow for differences in management efficiency or market conditions.

It is therefore clear that trying to determine the level at which profits can be considered supernormal is problematic and open to individual interpretation.

Market structures

As we saw earlier, the term 'market structure' refers to the characteristics of a market which determine a firm's conduct and behaviour. We will now look at the four main market structures in more detail.

PERFECTLY COMPETITIVE MARKET

A market is said to be perfectly competitive when "individually, buyers and sellers believe that their own actions will have no influence on the market price".

Perfectly competitive markets rarely exist in the real world, but agriculture, market gardening and the forex markets are good examples of them.

Characteristics of a perfectly competitive market

- In perfectly competitive markets there are a *large numbe*r of buyers and sellers who buy and sell such a small amount that they cannot affect market demand or supply.
- All firms in perfectly competitive markets produce *homogeneous* or identical products.
- In perfectly competitive markets there are *no barriers to entry*, which means that firms are free to enter and leave the industry as they wish.
- In perfectly competitive markets both buyers and sellers have *perfect knowledge* of market conditions. What this means is that all buyers and sellers know everything about all products in the market at all times, and therefore will always make the best decisions regarding production and purchase.

As a result of these characteristics, the perfectly competitive firm will be a **price-taker.** This means that firms in perfect competition have no control over the price they charge for their output. They must accept the market price as determined by the forces of demand and supply in the market, and sell all of their output at this market price.

What happens if the firm charges above the market price?

It will lose all its custom since consumers have perfect knowledge of prices elsewhere and will simply shift their demand to firms charging the market price. Furthermore, because the firm is such a small part of the overall industry it will have no incentive to lower price – it knows it can sell all its output at the market price. In other words, it will face a perfectly elastic demand curve.

Profits in perfectly competitive markets

Firms which operate in perfectly competitive markets are able to make abnormal profits in the short run. However, due to the fact that there is perfect knowledge in the industry, other firms will see this firm making abnormal profits, and as there are no barriers to entry, they will enter the industry and produce the same product until only normal profits are made by every firm. Therefore, in the long run, firms in perfect competition are only able to make normal profits.

ACTIVITY 3.1

Dairy farming: A perfectly competitive market?

Milk is a product we all take for granted. Almost every household in Northern Ireland buys milk on a regular basis, but how many of us ever consider how the product is produced and sold?

Most people in Northern Ireland buy milk which is either full cream or semi-skimmed. An increasing number of people now buy their milk in four-pint plastic bottles in supermarkets when they do their weekly shopping, with a decreasing amount of milk being delivered to the doorstep by milkmen.

The price of a pint of milk has not changed significantly in the last 10 years, even though the demand for milk is relatively price inelastic over a certain price range. The price that the dairy farm receives is only a fraction of the actual price paid by consumers. A litre of milk typically costs the consumer about 40p, but the dairy farm receives only 8p per litre.

The table below shows the number and size of dairy farms in Northern Ireland from 1993 to 2003.

	1993	2003
Total number of dairy farms	6,179	4,742
Total number of dairy cows (thousands)	273	291
Average herd size	44	61
Average milk yield per cow	4,930	6,290

Source: www.dardni.gov.uk

1. Use the information in the third paragraph to calculate what percentage of the price of a litre of milk is received by dairy farmers.
2. Explain what is meant by the statement "the demand for milk is relatively price inelastic over a certain price range".
3. What characteristics of a perfectly competitive market does the dairy farming industry possess?
4. How much influence would an individual dairy farm have on the price it charges for its milk?

COMPETITIVE MARKET

A competitive market is defined as "the market structure where there are a relatively large number of firms offering similar but differentiated products".

Competitive markets have some characteristics which are similar to perfect competition and some which are common to monopoly. The competitive market model is a more realistic model of the behaviour of firms in the real world, and examples of competitive industries include:

Donegall Place, Belfast

- pubs, clubs and hotels in a city centre
- chip shops
- clothes shops and shoe shops
- estate agents
- local builders/plumbers

Characteristics of a competitive market

- In a competitive market there are a *relatively large* number of buyers and sellers.
- The firms in a competitive market sell *differentiated* products – the goods are not perfect substitutes for each other and they are differentiated through **branding**. The more similar the products, the more elastic the demand curve.
- In competitive markets there is freedom of entry and exit into and out of the market. In other words, there are *no barriers to entry*. This means that a firm will only be able to make normal profits in the long run.
- The buyers and sellers have *imperfect knowledge* of the market. For example, imagine how difficult it would be to try and determine the price, quality and reliability of every plumber in the *Yellow Pages*.

Since firms in competitive markets produce products which are slightly different from those of their competitors, they will have a certain amount of market power and will have some influence over the price at which they sell their products. Therefore, firms in competitive markets will not be price-takers, since they have some market power. However, because there are a large number of firms producing similar products, this market power will be small, and the demand curve facing each firm will be relatively elastic.

Profits in competitive markets

In the short run it is possible for the competitive firm to make abnormal profits, but since there are no barriers to entry new firms will enter the industry until only normal profits are made by each firm.

When new firms enter the industry they increase the supply of similar products. This decreases the demand for each individual firm's products and therefore the demand curve for each firm shifts inwards and also becomes more elastic. This increase in the supply of similar products puts downward pressure on prices until eventually only normal profits are made by each firm.

ACTIVITY 3.2

The Belfast hotel market

A simple internet search for hotels in Belfast produces a result which lists over 50 hotels in the Belfast area. Some of these hotels are owned by large hotel groups and have accommodation for up to 200 people, with a number of bars and restaurants available on site. Others are much smaller family-owned businesses, with only a few rooms and limited entertainment.

The hotel industry is thriving at the moment. Tens of thousands of visitors stay in Belfast each year, and typically over 60% of all available rooms are booked.

1. Explain how one hotel might differentiate its product from that of its rivals.
2. What characteristics of a competitive market does the hotel industry possess?

The Europa Hotel, Belfast

OLIGOPOLY

An oligopolistic market is defined as "the market structure where the supply of a good or service is dominated by a few producers, each of whom has some control over the market". The Competition Commission further defines it as "the market structure where the top four firms have more than 60% of the market". Oligopoly is often simply referred to as "competition among the few".

Oligopolistic markets are quite common in reality, and examples include:

- petrol retailing and production: BP, Shell, ExxonMobil
- the chemical industry
- the telecommunications industry: BT, Virgin Media (previously NTL)
- the Northern Ireland banking market: Ulster Bank, First Trust, Bank of Ireland, and the Northern Bank

The Riverside Tower (BT Tower), Belfast

Characteristics of an oligopolistic market

- In oligopolistic markets, supply is concentrated in the hands of *relatively few* firms.

- Firms produce similar products, which are *differentiated* through branding.
- *Barriers to entry* exist and therefore firms will be able to continue making abnormal profits in the long run.
- There is *imperfect knowledge* in the industry. Consider trying to determine the rates of interest paid and the fees charged in all the different financial products offered by the four main banks in Northern Ireland.

Since firms in oligopolistic markets produce products which are differentiated from those of their competitors, they will have a certain amount of market power and will have some influence over the price at which they sell their products. Therefore, firms in oligopolistic markets will not be price-takers. However, because there are other firms producing similar products this market power will be limited. How much market power the oligopolistic firm has depends on its success in convincing the consumer that its product or service is different to that of its rivals.

Profits in oligopolistic markets

If one firm in an oligopolistic market is making abnormal profits, entrepreneurs may see these profits and attempt to enter the industry to gain some of the available profit. However, due to the fact that barriers to entry exist in the industry they are unable to do so, and therefore the oligopolistic firm can continue to make these abnormal profits in the long run.

ACTIVITY 3.3

The music industry

The market for the recording, sale and distribution of popular music is becoming increasingly concentrated as a result of a number of high-profile mergers and takeovers in the last five years.

Although there are many thousands of small independent record labels in the UK, the market could still be described as oligopolistic. The vast majority of successful recording artists have deals with the five main music companies, and many of the so-called independent labels have commercial ties with "the Big Five".

The chart opposite shows the market share enjoyed by the main recording companies in the UK.

1. Explain what is meant by the term 'oligopoly'.
2. What characteristics of an oligopolistic market does the music industry possess?
3. Why might further concentration in the UK music industry be bad for consumers?

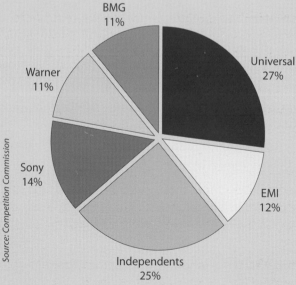

Source: Competition Commission

BMG 11%
Universal 27%
Warner 11%
Sony 14%
EMI 12%
Independents 25%

Competition in oligopolistic markets

Studies of oligopolistic markets have shown that prices are often very stable and tend not to change significantly, even when demand or supply conditions change.

Consider the music industry, for example. The price of a CD has not changed significantly over the last ten years, even though production costs have fallen and demand has fallen as a result of the growth of the MP3 market.

One possible reason for price stability in oligopolistic markets is that there might be an accepted price leader in the industry or what economists call a **barometric leader**. Any price changes in the industry would be initiated by the leader, and then other firms would follow suit.

There is evidence of price leadership in many industries, where smaller firms wait for the larger firms to initiate a price change and then they take similar action.

Another possible explanation of the relative price stability in oligopoly is that oligopolistic firms might reach a **collusive agreement**. A collusive agreement (or **collusion**) occurs when rival firms agree to set a common price or common conditions of sale in an attempt to manage the level of competition in a market. Collusion is illegal in the UK and European Union (EU), but it is very difficult to prove.

Price wars – whilst prices in oligopolistic markets often appear to be stable, at other times they can be highly unstable.

Sometimes firms in these markets engage in **price wars**. This occurs when one firm cuts prices very low in an attempt to destroy its rivals and gain their market share. It is a common strategy when demand for a product or service is falling.

For example, in the mid 1990s the *Mirror* newspaper initiated a price war with the other tabloids in an attempt to increase market share. It initially cut its price from 38p to 20p, but the *Sun* soon followed suit cutting its price to 20p. Both papers lost money as a result, and the *Mirror* was forced to increase its price back to its original level.

Non-price competition – the existence of price wars is evidence of competition in oligopolistic markets. However, this does not mean there is no competition when prices are stable. Non-price competition between firms in oligopoly is often intense. This refers to all forms of competition other than through the price mechanism.

Examples of non-price competition include branding, advertising, product placement, product endorsement, free gifts and promotions.

Why do firms use non-price competition?

One reason for using non-price competition is that firms find their cost structures are very similar, leaving little scope to compete on the basis of price. For example, consider the costs faced by sport retailers like JD Sports and JJB Sports. Both sell a similar range of branded goods, both have stores in towns and cities, and the wages and other running costs are likely to be similar for both firms.

Firms also tend to avoid price competition because they fear it may lead to price wars. They therefore tend to keep prices unchanged and compete in other ways.

In some cases firms simply believe that consumers are more sensitive to changes in style or quality rather than changes in price. This is typical in the clothing industry, and so clothes retailers tend to compete in these areas, rather than on price.

MONOPOLY

A monopolistic market is defined as "the market structure where there is a single seller of a good or service with no close substitute".

This kind of pure monopoly is actually very rare in reality, as most firms will face some competition. However, this does not mean that monopolies do not exist. In Northern Ireland there are a number of firms which produce almost all of the output in their industry and so should still be considered monopolies. For example, Northern Ireland Electricity (NIE) could be described as being a monopoly as it is the only company in Northern Ireland with a licence to generate and supply electricity.

If one large firm dominates an industry then it can still be regarded by economists as being a monopoly. Even if it faces competition from other firms it will still have significant monopoly power. The Competition Commission defines a monopoly as any firm having more than 25% market share. Using this definition the supermarket chain Tesco could be described as a monopoly since it has a 29% share of the UK grocery market.

The Competition Commission also has a stronger definition for a firm which dominates an industry. It defines a **dominant firm** as any firm having more than 40% market share. Microsoft would be described as being a dominant firm since it has a 90% share of the UK computer operating systems market (source: ONS).

Characteristics of a monopolistic market

- There is only *one* firm which sells all the output in the industry.
- The product or service is *unique* to the monopolist and has no close substitutes with which to compare it.
- *Barriers to entry* exist which keep would-be competitors from entering the market. Therefore, monopolistic firms will be able to make abnormal profits in the long run.

These characteristics mean that the monopolist will have a significant amount of market power and will therefore be able to set the price at which its products are sold. For this reason, monopolists are often referred to as **price-makers**.

However, it should be remembered that the power of the monopolist is not absolute since it is still constrained by the demand curve. In other words, if the monopolist decides to increase its price it must be willing to accept that there will be a reduction in the quantity demanded.

Profits in monopolistic markets

If the monopolistic firm is making abnormal profits, entrepreneurs may see these profits and attempt to enter the industry to gain some of the available profit. However, due to the fact that barriers to entry exist in the industry they are unable to do so, and therefore the monopolistic firm can continue to make these abnormal profits in the long run.

When describing market structures, be careful not to confuse *monopoly* with *monopolistic competition*. The term 'monopolistic market' is used to describe a market which is dominated by a monopoly, whereas the term 'monopolistically competitive market' or simply 'competitive market' is used to describe an industry which meets the criteria for monopolistic competition.

ACTIVITY 3.4

The market for computers

The computer market is often quoted as a good example of a monopolistic market. Monopolies are said to exist in both the manufacture of computers and in the market for computer software.

In the computer hardware market Dell is the preferred choice of the Northern Ireland consumer, and in the software market research has shown that Microsoft is the largest company, with its Windows™ operating system being used on over 80% of Northern Ireland's computers (source: OFT).

The table below gives the market share of the major computer manufacturers.

Computer manufacturer	Market share (2006)
Dell	31%
HP	19%
IBM	6%
Apple	6%
Others	38%

Source: www.oft.gov.uk

1. Using the information in the table above, state which firm could be described as having a monopoly in the manufacture of computers.
2. Explain why some economists might consider the market for computers in Northern Ireland as being oligopolistic.
3. Explain why Microsoft could be described as having a dominant position in the Northern Ireland software market.
4. Explain why monopoly power is regarded as being bad for consumers.

The degree of competition and its effects on consumers

The degree of competition in an industry will have a significant impact on the conduct of firms operating in that industry, but it will also have significant effects on the wider economy.

Most economists consider high levels of competition to be beneficial to an economy and it is these benefits that we will now consider.

However, it should also be remembered that high levels of competition can have some detrimental effects on the economy. These negative effects of competition will be considered in more detail in Chapter 5.

☐ THE BENEFITS OF COMPETITION

Having a significant degree of competition between firms in an industry will lead to benefits in four key areas.

Price

The level of competition will have a huge impact on the price that consumers pay for the output produced by an industry.

As a general rule those firms which face limited competition will have greater scope to influence their price and will therefore charge higher prices.

Those who face competition from a large number of firms producing similar products will have less scope to influence price and will, as a result, charge lower prices.

Quality

The level of competition in an industry will also have a significant impact upon the quality of goods and services produced by that industry.

Firms which face limited competition will have little incentive to maintain quality and may therefore produce poor quality goods and services.

On the other hand, firms which face a lot of competition will be forced to produce high quality goods for fear of losing their customers to competitors.

Choice

A lack of competition in a market can also lead to a lower level of choice for consumers. In those markets where output is produced by a sole supplier, consumers have no choice over where to purchase their product. However, in markets where there is significant competition the consumer may be able to choose from a range of differentiated products.

Efficiency

In highly concentrated industries firms with significant market power are in a position to charge prices which are considerably higher than would be the case in highly competitive markets. There will therefore be less incentive to introduce cost-saving innovations since the firm can respond to higher costs by simply raising prices. Consequently, organisational slack and inefficiency are common in markets with limited competition.

On the other hand, firms which face a lot of competition will be forced to become efficient if they wish to remain competitive.

Competition policy in the UK

The UK government attempts to control the degree of competition in markets through competition policy. It has passed a number of laws aimed at encouraging greater competition in markets. These include the Fair Trading Act, the Competition Act, the Restrictive Trade Practices Act, and more recently the Enterprise Act. These laws are all designed to stop large firms abusing their market power, and to try and make UK industry more competitive.

☐ WHO ENFORCES THESE LAWS?

The Office of Fair Trading (OFT)

The OFT carries out the initial investigations into company behaviour, and if it believes that action is required to improve competition it will refer the case to the Competition Commission.

The Competition Commission

This is an independent public body which carries out investigations into monopolies and **mergers**. It was established by the Competition Act 1998 and replaced the Monopolies and Mergers Commission on 1 April 1999.

Since the introduction of the Enterprise Act in 2002 the Commission has been responsible for making decisions on competition questions and for implementing appropriate remedies. Previously it could only make recommendations to the secretary of state who then decided whether or not to implement them.

The Enterprise Act also changed the Commission's terms of reference. Previously the Commission had to determine whether matters were *against the public interest*. It now concentrates specifically on competition grounds – judging each case on the impact it will have on competition.

The Commission states that its main aim is to increase the level of competition in the UK economy, and by doing so it aims to improve the UK's economic performance and productivity in the international economy.

Industry watchdogs

All of the major privatised utilities have an industry regulator, such as:

- The Office of Communication (Ofcom) for the communications industry, including internet, television and radio
- The Office of Rail Regulation (ORR) for railways
- The Office of Water Services (Ofwat) for water
- In Northern Ireland, the Office for the Regulation of Electricity and Gas (Ofreg) – in Britain this is known as the Office of Gas and Electricity Markets (Ofgem)

These watchdogs have the power to limit the share of the market one firm can control and they can impose price controls on firms. In practice this means that the watchdogs have the power to limit the price that firms, in the industries they regulate, can charge.

 ANTI-COMPETITIVE PRACTICES

The UK competition authorities are concerned with mergers and monopolies. They are also concerned with large firms which may not technically constitute a monopoly but which are large enough to have some power over the market. For example, if a group of companies together have more than 25% of the market and they adopt similar practices which restrict trade, they can then be classified as a **complex monopoly** and be dealt with as a monopoly.

The competition authorities also try to ensure that these firms do not abuse their market position by using anti-competitive practices. These are strategies used by producers with the aim of restricting competition in the market.

Examples of anti-competitive practices include the following.

Destroyer/predatory pricing

This occurs when a dominant firm cuts prices so low that other firms have to make a loss in order to match the low price. The aim of destroyer pricing is to force competitors out of the market and therefore strengthen the firm's monopoly position. For more information on destroyer/predatory pricing, see page 52.

Dominant display conditions

Large manufacturers often refuse to supply a retailer unless the retailer agrees to display the product in a prominent position at the expense of a rival firm's products. A prominent soft drinks company has been accused of using this strategy in Northern Ireland's main supermarkets.

Price fixing

This occurs when competitors agree to maintain prices within a certain limited range so as to avoid competition on the basis of price. Ultimately consumers suffer as price fixing tends to result in higher prices.

Resale price maintenance

This occurs where a manufacturer and a retailer agree that the retailer will sell the good at or above a pre-agreed price. Resale price maintenance prevents retailers from competing on the basis of price and therefore increases the profits of both the retailer and the manufacturer.

The EU and competition law

UK competition policy is designed to deal with issues which relate specifically to UK firms. The EU competition authorities, on the other hand, have policies and regulations which are designed to deal with competition issues affecting the EU. For example, the merger of a French company with a UK company may not be a cause for concern for the UK Competition Commission but it may be for the EU competition authorities.

©iStockphoto.com/dem10

Articles 85 and 86 of the **Treaty of Rome** forbid any activity which limits trade between EU member states. For example, the merger which took place between Bass Ireland and Interbrew was initially forbidden by the EU on competition grounds, as the new merged company would have had more than 25% of the EU market.

Concentration ratios

If the market leaders own a large proportion of the market, it is described as highly concentrated. By contrast, where the market leaders have a small proportion of the market, it can be described as highly competitive.

Concentration ratios are a method of measuring the degree of concentration in an industry. They can be based on a range of variables, including the total volume of output in the industry or the total value of output produced.

Concentration ratios are used by the Competition Commission to determine if an industry is monopolistic, oligopolistic or competitive.

☐ AGGREGATE CONCENTRATION RATIO

The aggregate concentration ratio takes the leading firms in an industry, for example the top five, and measures the *volume* of output they account for in that industry.

In Northern Ireland's construction industry the top five firms account for only 4% of total output (source: OFT), and so this industry could be described as highly competitive. It is based on the *value* of output.

MARKET CONCENTRATION RATIO

The market concentration ratio refers to the proportion of the market that is owned by the leading brands or companies in the market – for example, it measures how much of total output the top 5, 10 or 15 firms produce.

For example, in the sugar market the two largest firms (Tate & Lyle and British Sugar) account for over 70% of the market, so it could be described as highly concentrated.

Concentration ratios can also be calculated for other variables, for example the employment concentration ratio would measure the percentage of total employment taken by the top five firms.

The degree of concentration will help to tell us what type of market structure we are dealing with.

- If the top four firms account for more than 60% of the market then we would class it as oligopolistic.
- If one firm had more than 25% of the market share then we would class that firm as a monopolist.
- If one firm had more than 40% market share then it would be regarded as having a dominant position.

REVISION QUESTIONS

1. Explain, with examples, what is meant by the term 'barriers to entry'.
2. Explain the main features of a perfectly competitive market.
3. Explain why the forex market is considered by some to be a good example of a perfectly competitive market.
4. Explain the difference between normal and abnormal profits.
5. Explain the main features of a competitive market and give two examples of such a market.
6. Explain how firms in competitive markets differentiate their products from that of their rivals.
7. How does the Competition Commission determine if a market is oligopolistic?
8. Explain why oligopolistic firms tend to compete on the basis of non-price factors rather than on the basis of price.
9. Distinguish between a monopoly and a dominant firm.
10. Explain why consumers are believed to benefit from competition between firms.
11. Examine the role played by the Competition Commission in UK competition policy.
12. Explain, with the aid of examples, the term 'anti-competitive practices'.

CASE STUDY

Competition policy and Northern Ireland banks

Bank customers in Northern Ireland appear to be paying higher charges than those in Britain, a report has said.

The Competition Commission said it may be due to a lack of proper competition between "the Big Four" Northern Ireland banks. It said customers may be paying higher charges and getting lower rates of interest than they should.

(Adapted from BBC News website, 28 April 2006)

"The Big Four" banks (Northern Bank, Bank of Ireland, First Trust and Ulster Bank) hold a combined market share of over 80%, meaning the market structure is a highly concentrated oligopolistic market. This high market concentration gives the four banks the power to push up customer charges, allowing the banks to earn abnormal profits.

The banks are able to earn these abnormal profits because there are significant barriers to entry into the banking sector.

The first factor which prevents new firms entering the Northern Ireland market is the cost of entry. A new bank would need to have enough finance to establish a wide network of branches, and to advertise sufficiently to attract an adequate number of customers.

Another barrier to entry is customer inertia. It is well known that people often do not bother to change their bank account, even though better deals may be on offer, because it is seen as time-consuming. In Northern Ireland people are more likely to divorce than to switch banks!

Finally, the recent security scares associated with online banking have acted to deter people from using internet banking. This has reduced the ability of internet banks to compete with the established banks.

Using the information above, answer the questions below.

1. The Northern Ireland banking market has been described as oligopolistic. Explain what this means.
2. Why might the existence of oligopolies be bad for consumers?
3. Why have other banks not been able to compete with "the Big Four" in Northern Ireland?
4. Explain the role the OFT and the Competition Commission could play in this case.
5. Explain what is meant by the term 'abnormal profit'.
6. Examine some of the ways in which an economist might determine whether a firm was making abnormal profits.
7. Examine some of the forms of non-price competition used by banks in Northern Ireland.

CHAPTER 4

Dealing with competition

In the previous chapter we learned how the level of competition in a market can impact upon the behaviour of firms and the power they have to influence the price at which they sell their products.

In this chapter we will look at the range of strategies firms use to try and manipulate the level of competition in the market so as to give them a greater degree of market power. We will also look at how these strategies impact upon the various stakeholders of the business.

Stakeholders

A stakeholder is any person or group of people having an interest (or stake) in the success of a business.

Stakeholders can be classified as either *internal* or *external*. Internal stakeholders are members of the company or organisation, whereas external stakeholders are not members but have an interest in the business and its activities.

The main internal and external stakeholders are shown in the table below.

Internal	External
Shareholders	Customers
Managers	Suppliers
Employees	Local community
	Government
	Pressure groups
	Competitors
	Creditors
	Environment

All of the groups in this table have an interest in the activities of the business organisation and therefore could be considered to be stakeholders.

☐ SHAREHOLDERS

The company's shareholders have an interest in the success and profitability of the business since the capital growth and dividend payments associated with their shares depend upon the success of the business.

☐ MANAGERS

The managers of the company will also have an interest in the success of the business since their jobs and salaries depend on the business being successful. In many cases the actual level of pay a manager receives depends on the business meeting certain targets with regard to sales, revenues or profits.

☐ EMPLOYEES

Clearly, employees are stakeholders since their wages depend on the firm remaining in business. If the business is not a success then the employees may find themselves unemployed as the business sheds workers to reduce costs.

☐ CUSTOMERS

The company's customers have a stake in the business since they will be interested in the price of the product, the quality of the product, and the standard of service received.

☐ SUPPLIERS

Those who supply the business with raw materials or essential services will also have an interest in its performance. If the company is a success then they are likely to get more orders or business from the company as a result.

☐ LOCAL COMMUNITY

The local community can be considered as stakeholders since they will have concerns about the impact the firm has on the local environment. They will also be concerned about the level of employment in the area and the degree to which the firm engages with social projects in the surrounding area.

☐ GOVERNMENT

The government has an interest in the success and profitability of the business since the more profitable the firm is, the more it will pay the government in corporation tax. Companies also contribute to the public purse through VAT and employers' National Insurance Contributions.

☐ PRESSURE GROUPS

A pressure group can be described as an organised group that seeks to influence the actions and decisions of a business or government. Pressure groups take many different forms and include trade unions, professional bodies like the British Medical Association (BMA), and environmental groups such as Greenpeace and Friends of the Earth. It is obvious that pressure groups have an interest in the running of businesses, since they have been created with the express intention of influencing the actions of businesses or governments.

☐ COMPETITORS

A company's competitors can be considered stakeholders since they will have a keen interest in the relative price and quality of the firm's product, as well has being concerned with the firm's market power in relation to their own.

☐ CREDITORS

The company's creditors can also be considered to have a stake in the success of the business. Creditors are people who are owed money by the firm, and include those who lent money to the business (**lenders**) and those who have supplied goods and services but have yet to receive payment. If a firm is successful then it is more likely to be able to pay its creditors in full and on time.

☐ ENVIRONMENT

Finally, many people consider the environment to be a key stakeholder in all business activity since most forms of production impact upon the environment in some way. Clearly the environment is unable to represent itself in any way, and therefore it often falls to environmental pressure groups to defend the interests of the environment.

ACTIVITY 4.1

Stakeholders and John Lewis

The up-market department store chain John Lewis has decided to open a new store at the Sprucefield retail park outside Lisburn.

The development is expected to create up to 1,000 full and part-time jobs, with work expected to begin in 2007. The retailer is run as a partnership, with employees receiving a bonus based on the size of the company's profits.

Lisburn DUP councillor Edwin Poots said it was a coup for the city: "The store will draw thousands of people from outside the area".

(Adapted from BBC News website, 29 June 2004)

However, retailers in Belfast city centre are unhappy at the announcement, claiming it contravenes Northern Ireland planning policy.

List the main stakeholder groups for John Lewis and for each explain how they will be affected by the company's decision to open a retail outlet at Sprucefield.

John Lewis flagship store, Oxford Street, London

Managing competition

The vast majority of firms in Northern Ireland face competition from firms selling similar products. This competition could be from other UK firms or, increasingly, from foreign firms which may have lower costs.

ACTIVITY 4.2

For each of the firms below try to name two competitors. If possible, try to name one from the UK and one from abroad.

1. Coca-Cola
2. Tayto
3. Tesco
4. Ryanair

This competition means that firms must look for ways to manage the competition they face in the market so as to give them a greater degree of market power. Broadly speaking, there are two main approaches that a firm can use to deal with the competition it faces.

The first approach is for the firm to try and reduce the level of competition they have to deal with through taking over, amalgamating or merging with one of its rivals. If a firm merges with or takes over one of its rivals then it will no longer have to compete with them. Therefore, its market power should increase as a result.

The second approach is for the firm to try to become more competitive. If a firm can become more competitive in terms of price or quality, then it can ensure consumers will continue to buy its product rather than that of its rivals.

MANAGING COMPETITION THROUGH MERGERS OR ACQUISITIONS

The Competition Commission defines a merger as occurring when "two or more firms cease to be distinct". A merger happens when two firms agree to join together to form one larger company, whereas an **acquisition** occurs when one firm takes over or buys another firm.

Takeovers can be classified as **hostile** or **friendly**. A friendly takeover occurs whenever the bidder informs the target of its intention to acquire it. If the board of directors feels that the bid represents good value for the shareholders they will recommend acceptance of the bid. If not, the board will reject the bid and therefore the takeover attempt will be classified as hostile. In addition, if the bidder makes the initial bid without first informing the board it will also be considered to be hostile.

In the UK, takeovers and mergers are strictly regulated by the City Code on Takeovers and Mergers and the EU directive on takeovers.

Mergers can also be classified as **horizontal**, **vertical** or **conglomerate**.

Horizontal integration

This occurs when two firms which produce similar products merge. The firms must be at the same stage of production in the same industry. Examples of horizontal integration include the merger of Halifax and the Bank of Scotland to form HBOS in 2001, and the takeover in 2006 of Grove Services by its main competitor Maybin.

Vertical integration

This occurs when two firms in the same industry merge, but the two firms are at different stages in the production process. There are two types of vertical integration.

Backwards – vertical backwards integration occurs when a company takes over a firm supplying its raw materials, for example a pub buying a brewery. A high profile example of a vertical backwards merger was the purchase of Time Warner in 2001 by the internet service provider AOL.

Forwards – vertical forwards integration occurs when a firm takes over a company further along the production chain, for example a brewery buying a pub.

Essentially, if a company takes over another company which is further back in the production chain and therefore closer to the source of raw materials, then it is described as vertical backwards. However, if a company takes over another company which is further forward in the production chain and therefore closer to the final consumer, then it is described as vertical forwards.

Conglomerate integration

This occurs when firms in different industries merge. The goods and services they produce are not directly related. An example of a conglomerate takeover would be the merger of a cheese-processing plant with an electronics manufacturer.

The term 'conglomerate' is used to describe a company that is made up of a number of unrelated businesses. An example of a conglomerate is Quinn Group which has a range of businesses operating in diverse industrial sectors such as quarrying and cement manufacture, financial services, and hospitality.

The various different types of integration are illustrated in the diagram below.

Slieve Russell Hotel, County Cavan, owned by Quinn Group

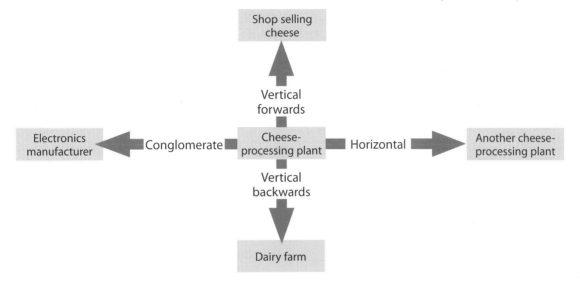

ACTIVITY 4.3

Classifying mergers

Classify each of the following examples of integration as either horizontal, vertical backwards, vertical forwards or conglomerate.

1. Two dentists merge into a single practice.
2. A computer software company takes over a firm producing soft drinks.
3. Tayto purchases Golden Wonder.
4. Coca-Cola merges with C&C.
5. A clothing manufacturer purchases a clothes shop.
6. An oil refinery purchases a number of petrol forecourts.
7. A supermarket purchases a food-processing plant.
8. Halifax merges with Bank of Scotland.
9. Disney purchases Pixar.

Benefits of managing competition through mergers and acquisitions

Expanding a firm through merger and acquisition can lead to a number of benefits for the business. These benefits include the following.

Economies of scale – merging with or acquiring another firm will allow a company to grow quickly and therefore gain economies of scale. Economies of scale are those advantages that large firms have over small firms which lead to falling average costs. For example, large firms are able to purchase their raw materials in bulk and therefore secure discounts. For more information on economies of scale, see pages 49–50.

Diversification – expanding a firm, particularly through vertical or conglomerate integration, will enable it to diversify its output and will therefore help to reduce the risk of changes to demand conditions. If the demand for one product falls then the firm can rely on sales of the other products to secure profits.

Market power – expanding a firm through horizontal integration will automatically increase its market share and will therefore also increase its market power. This increase in market power may allow the firm to increase price and profitability.

Gain of specialist knowledge – merging with another company allows a firm to bring new skills and specialised departments into the business which will complement the skills and expertise of the original business.

Drawbacks of managing competition through mergers and acquisitions

The completion of a merger or takeover is no guarantee of success. Indeed, expanding the firm through merger and acquisition can lead to a number of difficulties and can sometimes cause a net loss in value rather than a gain. Experience would seem to suggest that a large number of mergers do in fact result in a loss of value to the acquiring company.

The difficulties created through merging include the following.

Diseconomies of scale – merging with or acquiring another firm may lead a company to grow too large too quickly and therefore experience diseconomies of scale. Diseconomies of scale are those disadvantages of increased size which lead to increasing average costs. For example, large firms often experience managerial problems with regard to communication channels and staff motivation, and therefore the firm becomes less efficient and average costs increase as a result. For more information on diseconomies of scale, see page 50.

©iStockphoto.com/Renphoto

Incompatible corporate cultures – different companies have different cultures and different ways of getting things done. Bringing two firms together can cause these two cultures to clash, meaning resources have to be diverted away from new investment or research and development towards measures to correct the conflict.

Lack of expertise – when a firm merges with or takes over a firm which operates in another industry it may lack the specific expertise needed to be a success in that industry. This problem is often exacerbated by the laying off of key personnel in an attempt to achieve **synergies** or economies of scale. The term 'synergies' refers to the reduction in administrative costs which are expected when two firms merge.

Attracting of regulation – expanding a firm through horizontal integration leads to an increase in the market share enjoyed by the merged firm. However, if this market share becomes too large it may lead to an investigation by the competition authorities which can be both expensive and time-consuming.

ACTIVITY 4.4

Adidas rues cost of Reebok woes

German sports group Adidas has cut its forecast for profit growth in 2007 as a result of plans to spend more money on revamping its ailing US arm, Reebok.

Adidas, the second-largest sports firm worldwide after US firm Nike, cut its forecast for net income growth from 20% to 15% for 2007.

The news sent its shares down 8%, the biggest drop on Germany's DAX index (an index of the top 30 German stocks).

Adidas bought Reebok in 2005 because it believed the acquisition would boost its trade in the US, but recent figures show Reebok sales have fallen.

"Reebok's orders are disappointing and the outlook is lacklustre. It will take longer to put Reebok on track," said Nils Lesser, an analyst with Merck Finck.

Adidas reported a net loss of four million euros ($4.8m; £2.74m), blaming the costs of its takeover of Reebok.

The fourth-quarter loss compares with a net profit of 20 million euros a year earlier, and was worse than forecasts had predicted.
(Adapted from BBC News website, 2 March and 9 November 2006)

1. How would you classify the merger which took place between Adidas and Reebok in 2006?
2. Give three possible reasons why Adidas might have wanted to acquire Reebok.
3. Why might the merger between Adidas and Reebok not have been as successful as was hoped?

Economies of scale

As stated earlier, economies of scale are those advantages of increased size which lead to falling average costs.

They constitute one of the main reasons why firms wish to grow. The larger the firm becomes the greater the economies it can take advantage of and the lower its costs will be.

If the firm can take advantage of these economies of scale then it will be able to reduce price and therefore increase the demand for its product at the expense of its competitors. On the other hand, if the firm has few competitors then it will be able to keep price constant and increase its profit margins. Either way, the firm is better off if it can avail of economies of scale.

There are many sources of economies of scale, including the following.

Technical economies – large firms can take advantage of increased-capacity machinery, which allows faster and more efficient production.

Mass production also allows specialisation and division of labour, which enables the firm to increase output at little extra cost.

Marketing economies – large firms can buy their raw materials in bulk and therefore get discounts. In addition, since advertising costs are spread over a larger level of output, average advertising costs are reduced.

Financial economies – large firms can get loans at lower rates of interest because they are more creditworthy. Their average costs are consequently lower.

Managerial economies – large firms can employ specialist managers, accountants and salespeople, whereas in small firms one person may have to fill many roles. These specialist workers will increase the productivity of the firm.

©iStockphoto.com/marck75

Diseconomies of scale

However, when a firm becomes too large it may actually find that its average costs increase. When this happens the firm is experiencing diseconomies of scale. As stated earlier, diseconomies of scale are those disadvantages of increased size which lead to rising average costs.

Diseconomies of scale can occur for a number of reasons. However, they are normally the result of management problems, such as the following.

Coordination – large firms often find it difficult to coordinate the work of a whole range of different sections. In consequence, firms may find that at certain times some workers are not working as hard as they could be because they are waiting for other people to finish their work before they can start. This obviously increases a firm's costs since these workers still have to be paid.

Control – keeping an eye on every worker in a large organisation is often very difficult, so slack or what economists term **X-inefficiency** may occur.

Cooperation – large firms often find that worker morale is quite low, resulting in reduced labour productivity.

Firms will therefore attempt to grow to take advantage of economies of scale, but they will not want to grow too large for fear of diseconomies of scale setting in.

Case study: Small and medium-sized enterprises (SMEs)

As large firms experience many cost advantages over smaller firms, there is often the desire for small firms to grow quickly (either through internal expansion or through mergers) in order to gain these economies of scale.

Despite this, SMEs still make up a significant part of the economies of Britain and Northern Ireland.

What is an SME?

Businesses can be classified as small, medium-sized or large, either on the basis of the number of employees they have or their turnover. The Department of Trade and Industry (DTI) classifies business size according to the number of employees:

- Micro firm: 0–9 employees
- Small firm: 0-49 employees (includes micro)
- Medium firm: 50–249 employees
- Large firm: over 250 employees

The EU classifies business size according to both the head count (number of employees) and turnover.

Enterprise category	Head count	Turnover (€)
Micro	<10	<2 million
Small	<50	<10 million
Medium	<250	<50 million

How important are SMEs to the economies of Northern Ireland and Britain?

The DTI estimates that of the 4.3 million business enterprises in the UK, 99.9% were small to medium-sized and that these SMEs account for about 58% of all UK employment.

In Northern Ireland SMEs account for nearly 80% of employment, with about 50% of businesses being classified as micro businesses.

Why do SMEs make up such a significant part of the economies of Northern Ireland and Britain?

- In some industries diseconomies of scale exist at relatively low levels of output. This encourages the firms to remain small.
- In personal services, for example hairdressing, there are very few economies of scale and so the desire to grow is non-existent.
- Small firms are often more flexible and better able to adapt to changes in market conditions, meaning they often survive even when larger firms go under.
- Many small firms exist because they supply specialist goods or services for niche markets where demand is relatively low, for example paraffin lamps, surfboards and bodhráns.
- Many firms remain small because they supply only a local market. In the UK there are a large number of small breweries which supply pubs in their local area. These breweries do not expand beyond their local area because of the extremely high transport costs associated with a bulky product like alcohol.
- In a dynamic economy like the UK new firms are starting up all the time as market opportunities arise. By their very nature new firms tend to be small.
- The UK government actively encourages the development of new firms, through business start-up grants and tax breaks for small firms. In Northern Ireland this role is carried out by Invest Northern Ireland.

MANAGING COMPETITION THROUGH IMPROVED COMPETITIVENESS

As stated earlier, an alternative approach used by firms to deal with competition is for the firm to try to become more competitive. A firm becomes more competitive when it can ensure that consumers will continue to buy its products rather than that of its rivals.

If a firm can gain a competitive advantage over its rivals then the firm can grow **organically**. Organic growth occurs whenever a firm grows naturally through increasing sales and market share as opposed to merging with or acquiring another firm.

There are a number of strategies a firm can use to become more competitive, including competing on price and competing on product.

Competing on price (becoming price competitive)

The most obvious way a firm can become more competitive is by reducing its prices. We learned in Chapter 2 how a reduction in price would lead to an increase in quantity demanded of the good or service. We also learned that if the demand was price elastic then this reduction in price would also lead to an increase in total revenue.

Before engaging in price-cutting strategies firms will often look for ways to reduce their costs to ensure they maintain their profit margins. Firms can reduce their costs through increasing labour and capital technology, through increases in efficiency, or through investing in new technologies.

There are two main problems with price cutting as a strategy for dealing with competition. The first is that it could lead to a price war, particularly if the industry is oligopolistic. As we learned earlier, a price war occurs whenever competing firms undertake a series of price reductions in an attempt to gain market share. When one firm reduces price the others follow suit and undercut their rivals. Price wars benefit consumers in the short run, but because they often lead to the closure of smaller firms, prices generally increase in the long run.

The second problem with competing on price, and one of the main reasons why firms are often reluctant to engage in price-cutting strategies, is that they fear the image and reputation of their product might suffer as a result.

Pricing strategies – if a firm is using price in an attempt to increase its competitiveness, it has a number of different pricing strategies to choose from. The following are the most common pricing strategies used by firms.

Destroyer/predatory pricing

This is when a firm sells its products at a very low price with the intention of driving competitors out of the market, or to create a barrier to entry to prevent potential competitors from entering the market. If the firm is able to drive competitors from the market it will be able to raise its prices again to a level above the original competitive level.

Predatory pricing is used by firms which have a degree of market power, and can be very successful in the long run. However, in the short run the firm may lose money as a result of this strategy, and if the competition is not as weak as predicted the firm engaging in this strategy may itself be forced out of the market.

Competitive pricing

This is when a firm sets its price at a level which is at or just below the price charged by its main competitors. The price is set at a rate which makes the goods appear competitive but at the same time does not have a detrimental impact on the image of the product.

Competitive pricing is a very common strategy and normally forms part of a wider promotional campaign.

The problem with this as a strategy for dealing with competition is that it could lead to a price war, which can be both risky and expensive for the business.

Penetration pricing

This is often used when a new product is being introduced onto a market which is already relatively competitive, and a firm sets a low initial entry price to attract consumers to the product. The price is then increased towards the market price as consumer loyalty is built up. Penetration pricing is only useful for goods which generate repeat purchases, and is often used in the market for magazines and confectionery.

This is a very effective way of maximising sales and works best when demand is price elastic. However, the low initial price associated with penetration pricing may be damaging to a product's reputation and may simply attract bargain hunters who will switch to another product whenever price increases.

Psychological pricing

This occurs when a firm sells a product at a price designed to convince the consumer that the product is cheaper than it really is. For example, when a product is sold at £39.99 consumers tend to ignore the 99p and subconsciously believe that the product is closer to £39 than £40. This is a very common strategy, with over 70% of all goods sold in the UK ending in either 99p or 95p.

Research has shown that psychological pricing is very effective and that consumers are more likely to round down than round up whenever prices end in odd numbers.

However, as with any pricing policy which makes the product appear cheaper than that of rival products, psychological pricing may be damaging to customers' preconceived views about the quality of the product.

Skimming/creaming

Skimming is often used by firms launching a new or improved product onto the market. The price of the product is set high initially to target those consumers who are likely to be willing to pay the higher price. These consumers are known as **early adopters** and are less sensitive to price.

©iStockphoto.com/Limber

Consider the market for plasma screen televisions. These products currently retail at very high prices, but early adopters are still keen to purchase the televisions and will be willing to pay the high price. After a period of time the price of these televisions will be reduced in an attempt to price other consumers into the market.

Skimming can be a very effective way of increasing sales revenue, but it will only be successful if the demand for the product is inelastic. Using a price-skimming strategy is also likely to draw competitors into the industry as they will be attracted by the high margins available.

Cost-plus pricing

This occurs when a firm calculates the average cost of producing a good or service and then adds on a percentage profit or mark-up to calculate the selling price. It is the most common form of pricing used by small firms and new businesses.

The problem with this strategy is that it takes no account of demand and therefore there is no way of knowing if potential customers will purchase the product at the calculated selling price.

Competing on the product

Due to the increased level of competition from countries such as China and India, which have very low wages, firms in Britain and Northern Ireland have been finding it increasingly difficult to compete on the basis of price. They have therefore begun to look for other ways in which to compete.

Improving quality – if the firm can improve the quality of its products then it can compete on the basis of quality rather than price. As incomes have increased, consumers have become more concerned with the quality of the goods and services they purchase than with the price, so if a firm can improve the quality of its products it can justify selling them at a higher price.

Adding value – adding value to a product is similar to improving the quality of the product but they are different strategies. Strategies which add value to a product do not necessarily improve its quality.

Adding value to a product simply means making it more desirable to consumers. For example, a potato producer could add value to their products by washing the potatoes before selling them. They could add further value by peeling, slicing, and cooking the potatoes. A car manufacturer could add value to a car by adding alloy wheels, a stereo system, and leather seats.

If the firm can add value to its products or services then it can sell them at a higher price.

Product differentiation – this means a firm modifying its product or service in an attempt to make it appear different to that of its rivals. The product is distinguished through the use of branding. The extent to which the goods and services of competing firms are different varies between industries, but often the differences are minor or superficial with differences in the packaging or promotions being the main focus.

iStockphoto.com/macroworld

Branding

> This simply refers to the process of giving a product its own identity. Branding a product reduces its PED and therefore allows the firm to increase price without any large reduction in quantity demanded.

> If a firm can build a strong brand and convince consumers that its products are superior to those of its rivals, then it will gain a clear competitive advantage and will therefore be able to continue selling its products, even if they are at a higher price.

Advertising

> This refers to the process of drawing attention to a product, brand or company. Advertising can take place across a range of media, for example television, radio, billboards, magazines and web pop-ups.

> Regardless of the form of media used to advertise a product, the objective of the advertisement remains the same, namely to *inform* consumers about the product and to *persuade* those consumers to purchase the product.

> As we saw in Chapter 2, an effective advertising campaign should lead to an increase in the demand for a product and should therefore make the firm more competitive. Indeed, in the modern economy advertising is one of the best methods a firm has of gaining a competitive advantage over its rivals.

REVISION QUESTIONS

1. List three internal and three external stakeholders and explain why they are stakeholders in a business.
2. How does the Competition Commission define the term 'merger'?
3. Distinguish between a friendly and a hostile takeover.
4. Explain, with examples, the difference between a horizontal and a vertical merger.
5. Explain what is meant by the term 'conglomerate'.
6. Explain what is meant by organic growth.
7. Explain what is meant by the term 'economies of scale', using examples to illustrate your answer.
8. Explain three reasons why SMEs make up such a large part of the Northern Ireland economy.
9. Distinguish between the following pricing policies:

   (a) Skimming
   (b) Penetration pricing
   (c) Predatory pricing

10. Explain what is meant by the term 'product differentiation'.
11. Explain how a firm could add value to its products.
12. What are the two main functions of advertising?

CASE STUDY

McDonald's facing competition
(Adapted from BBC News website, December 2006, and published accounts)

Fast-food chain McDonald's is closing 25 branches in a bid to improve profits at its struggling UK operations.

The closures were listed in McDonald's annual accounts, which showed that poor British sales were dragging down its profits.

This reduction in profits caused the company's share price to collapse from a high of $48 in 1999 to a low of just over $12 in 2005.

In the accounts, the firm said its UK stores were "experiencing a highly competitive informal eating-out market and low consumer confidence levels".

A source close to McDonald's stated that profits had been severely hit in the UK as a result of concerns about health, greater price competition from other fast-food restaurants, and the entrance into the market of gourmet sandwich stores.

Others in the industry suggest that McDonald's decline is a result of it becoming too big and less customer-focused. One industry insider stated that "McDonald's problems are of its own making. It has allowed its image and brand to become dated and as a result people are switching to cooler, more hip, restaurants which sell more exotic foods."

However, the company is not giving up. McDonald's chief executive Ralph Alvarez stated recently that "the world has changed; our customers have changed; we need to change too."

The plan to reverse the trend of falling sales includes the following.

- Costs will be cut by reducing the number of new restaurants opened from an average of 1,700 per year to around 350. This will slash capital spending and the money saved can be used to reduce the company's debt burden.
- Action will also be taken to improve management and staff productivity through monitoring standards.
- The image of the restaurants is to be improved through the introduction of a quality control system ensuring the maintenance of cleanliness and customer service standards.
- The menu is to be slimmed down, with a greater emphasis on healthy products such as salads and sliced fruit.
- Finally, the advertising focus is to receive an overhaul, with a greater emphasis on young adults.

Using the information above, answer the questions below.

1. Use the information in the third paragraph to calculate the percentage change in share price between 1999 and 2005.
2. Analyse three reasons why sales and profits at McDonald's have declined in recent years.
3. Explain why a fall in profits would also cause a fall in the share price of McDonald's.
4. What evidence does the article provide which suggests that McDonald's is operating in a competitive market?
5. McDonald's has an ambitious plan to reverse the decline in sales and profits. Critically evaluate how the strategies outlined in the plan would impact upon three of McDonald's stakeholders.

CHAPTER 5

Government influence and economic policy

In Chapter 3 we learned how the level of competition in a market could have a positive effect on the stakeholders of a business. We saw how higher levels of competition resulted in lower prices, higher quality goods and services, and greater levels of efficiency.

In this chapter we will learn how competition can also have a negative effect on the firm's stakeholders, and we will look at the policies the government can use to ensure the market system works well for everyone.

Negative effects of competition

Having a high level of competition between firms is generally regarded to be in the public interest, since firms are more likely to produce high quality goods at lower prices.

However, in an attempt to gain a competitive advantage over their rivals, firms may engage in activities which produce undesirable consequences for both the internal and external stakeholders.

These undesirable consequences can be illustrated by looking at the case studies below which have been taken from local and national newspapers during November 2006.

Case Study: Clothing company closes Derry plant

A major clothing company has announced the closure of its sewing operation in Londonderry with the loss of 150 jobs.

The firm said the reasons for the shutdown included the cost pressures on Ireland as a base coupled with substantial overproduction of certain garments for coming seasons.

A local trade union representative stated "The company has been shaving jobs over the last two years in the Republic [of Ireland]. But I had been told there would be no further jobs losses here in the next year."

More than 4,000 jobs have been lost in the textiles industry in the province over the last two years.

This first case study illustrates how increased levels of competition can lead to a *higher risk of unemployment* for some workers, with over 4,000 textile workers losing their jobs in two years as a result of increased levels of competition in this industry.

Experience would suggest that the greater the competition within an industry, the more likely a firm is to try and reduce costs in an attempt to remain competitive. While most people would consider this to be a positive step, it may have negative consequences for some employees. This is because one of the most common cost-cutting strategies used by firms is to reduce their workforce. This obviously has a detrimental impact upon the employees, and it also negatively affects other stakeholders such as the wider community and the government.

Case Study: Oil company has been fined £25,000 following a pollution alert in the North Sea

The firm was prosecuted after diesel gushed into the water as a supply vessel refuelled a platform about 160 miles east of Aberdeen.

It was a "routine operation", but 6.5 tonnes of fuel – intended to power the platform's generators – was discharged into the sea. The investigation found that "environmental best practice procedures for the transport of large quantities of oil were not being followed by the company".

A spokesman said the company "regretted" the accident. He added that the firm had carried out its own investigation, along with an inquiry conducted by the authorities.

The official stressed that the energy giant had learned lessons and "remedial action" had been taken in an effort to prevent a similar spill.

This case study illustrates how increased levels of competition can lead to *increased levels of pollution* and therefore have a negative effect on the local and national environment.

In an attempt to reduce costs, firms will use the cheapest method of production. However, as the case study demonstrates, the production process which has the lowest cost may not always be the most environmentally friendly.

©iStockphoto.com/vandervelden

Case Study: Solar heating firm fined £40,000 for cooking up lies

A solar heating firm has been fined £40,000 for exaggerating the benefits of "going green".

The firm claimed household energy bills would be slashed by 70% when the truth was just 8%. In the first prosecution of its kind in Britain, the £5 million a-year company was found guilty of misleading the public under the Trade Descriptions Act.

A spokesman for Dorset Trading Standards said "All we are asking is that firms like [these] stick to the facts so consumers can make a decision based on correct facts."

This case study illustrates how higher levels of competition can lead to an *increased risk of unfair trade.*

In a situation where consumers have imperfect knowledge about the qualities of a product, producers may be tempted to exaggerate or lie about the merits of their product in an attempt to secure a sale.

Case Study: Sportswear manufacturer condemned for using sweatshop labour

The international aid agency Oxfam Community Aid Abroad has released a new report condemning conditions at dozens of factories in Indonesia supplying a top sportswear manufacturer.

The report says tens of thousands of employees are still living in extreme poverty and work in dangerous conditions.

This case study illustrates the *social and ethical problems* associated with high levels of competition.

In an attempt to maintain a competitive advantage and raise profits in an increasingly competitive marketplace, firms may be tempted to move production to low-wage countries where labour laws are more relaxed than in the UK. Many of the high street's biggest names have been accused of sourcing their products from companies which use child labour or force employees to work in dangerous conditions.

These case studies highlight the main problems associated with increased levels of competition and illustrate the need for government policy to correct these problems.

Government intervention in the market

The government often intervenes in the market to protect the various stakeholders and to provide a healthy competitive environment in which business can prosper.

This government intervention can take various forms, from the introduction of regulations and laws to the imposition of taxes and other charges. The form this intervention takes depends on the reasons for the intervention and the nature of the market involved.

☐ ENSURING FAIR TRADE

One of the main reasons for government intervention in a market is to ensure fair trade in the market. We learned earlier in this chapter that some firms may be tempted to mislead consumers in an effort to secure higher profits. For this reason the UK government has passed a number of laws which protect consumers from unscrupulous traders, including the Sale of Goods Act, the Trade Descriptions Act, and the Weights and Measures Act.

☐ CONTROLLING COMPETITION

Another reason why governments intervene in a market is to control the level of competition, ensuring that individual firms do not gain too much market power.

We learned in Chapter 3 that the UK government has passed a number of laws aimed at encouraging greater competition in markets, including the Fair Trading Act, the Competition Act, the Restrictive Trade Practices Act, and more recently the Enterprise Act. These laws are all designed to make UK industry more competitive by preventing large firms from abusing their market power.

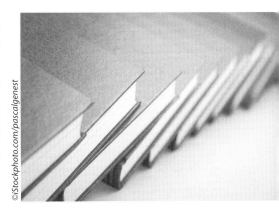

©iStockphoto.com/pascalgenest

☐ PROTECTING THE ENVIRONMENT

Another motive for government intervention in a market is to protect the environment from the pollution caused through either the production or the consumption of goods and services.

Firms which operate in competitive markets will generally seek to use the cheapest and most cost-effective method of production. However, as we saw in the second case study, the cheapest method of production may not always be the most environmentally friendly.

For this reason the government has introduced various pieces of legislation to protect the environment, for example the Clean Air Act and the Environmental Protection Act. It has also introduced a number of environmental taxes in an attempt to reduce pollution, including the Climate Change Levy and the excise duty on fuel.

☐ PROTECTING STAKEHOLDERS

Another reason why governments intervene in a market is to protect the various stakeholders from abuse.

We saw earlier how firms may be tempted to lay off workers or force employees to work in unsafe conditions in an attempt to reduce costs. To prevent this happening the government has introduced a number of pieces of legislation which protect employees from being poorly treated by their employers – for example the Fair Employment Act, the Equal Pay Act, and the Sex Discrimination Act.

Some of the more recent legislation, for example the National Minimum Wage and the Working Time Directive, has been introduced as a result of the UK government signing up to the social chapter of the Maastricht Treaty which has brought UK legislation into line with the rest of the EU.

☐ ACHIEVING MACROECONOMIC OBJECTIVES

One final motive for government intervention in the market is to create a stable, competitive economy. The government considers a stable and competitive economy to be one which has:

- Low levels of inflation
- Low levels of unemployment
- High but sustainable levels of economic growth
- An acceptable balance of payments

Achieving these macroeconomic objectives is the key to the government creating the conditions necessary for businesses to develop and prosper.

Low levels of inflation

Inflation is defined as a *sustained rise in the general level of prices*. The **inflation rate** is the annual percentage change in the general price level.

There are a number of different measures of inflation used in the UK, including the **RPI** (Retail Price Index) and the **RPI-X** (RPI minus mortgage interest payments). However, the official measure of inflation in the UK is through the use of the **CPI** (Consumer Price Index).

The CPI is a weighted index which measures the cost of living for a household with average spending patterns. The government creates a 'shopping basket' of 650 of the most commonly-consumed goods and services, and the retail price of these goods and services is measured in various regions of the UK. The basket is weighted to reflect the relative importance of each item and an index number is created which represents the cost of the basket of goods. This index number is compared with the index number of the same basket for the previous year and the annual rate of inflation is calculated.

The government measures inflation by all three methods, but the CPI has replaced the RPI-X as the government's preferred measure and it is the CPI inflation rate of 2% (+/- 1%) that the Bank of England must target.

☐ TRENDS IN INFLATION

The graph below shows the rate of inflation in the UK, as measured by the CPI, between 1997 and 2006. We can see from the graph that the UK inflation rate has been below the 2% target for much of the last nine years.

UK inflation rates 1997–2006

Source: ONS

☐ INFLATION AND DEFLATION

When inflation occurs this does not mean that the price of all goods is increasing. It means only that *on average* prices are increasing. Even when average prices as measured by the CPI are increasing, the price of some goods and services may actually be falling.

The chart below shows the main components of the CPI basket and the relative price changes over a one-month period. We can see that the price of some goods has increased, for example food and non-alcoholic beverages, while the cost of others, for example furniture and household goods, has fallen.

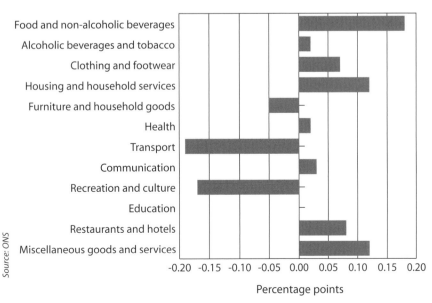

Percentage points

Source: ONS

☐ THE CAUSES OF INFLATION

Economists believe that inflation has two main causes.

Demand-pull inflation

This occurs when there is too much demand in an economy for too few goods.

If aggregate (total) demand in an economy is allowed to increase and the economy is nearing full employment, then the increase in aggregate demand is likely to lead to an increase in prices. This is shown in the diagram below.

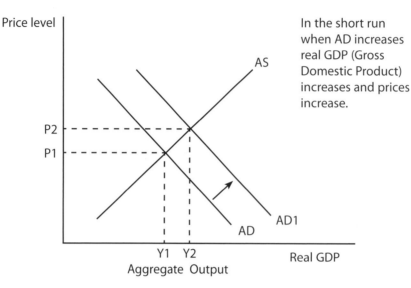

In the short run when AD increases real GDP (Gross Domestic Product) increases and prices increase.

Cost-push inflation

Some economists argue that inflation could also be cost-push in nature, as increases in the cost of raw materials would be passed on by firms in order to maintain profit margins.

For example, if oil prices increase most firms will find that the cost of production increases. This increase in costs shifts the aggregate supply curve to the left and causes an increase in prices, as shown on the diagram below.

©iStockphoto.com/araraadt

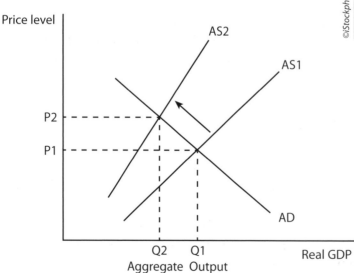

Cost-push inflation has many causes, including the following.

Increases in unit labour costs – if labour costs increase, for example as a result of increases to the National Minimum Wage, then firms will seek to pass on the increase in wages as an increase in price and therefore cause inflation.

Increased cost of raw materials – as stated earlier, if oil prices increase most firms will find that the cost of production increases. This increase in costs will shift the aggregate supply curve to the left and cause an increase in inflation.

Higher import prices – if the sterling exchange rate falls, the price of imports into the UK will increase. If firms import their raw materials they will find that they have increased costs and will therefore attempt to pass this increase in costs on as an increase in price.

Many economists argue that an increase in costs will start off a **cost-push spiral** which will lead to successively higher and higher rates of inflation. This is illustrated below.

Oil price increase   →   Leads to increased costs   Causes firms to increase price   Real incomes fall and people feel worse off   They ask for increased wages

WHY CONTROL INFLATION?

Governments aim to control inflation because it causes UK goods to become less competitive relative to foreign-made goods. Therefore, the demand for UK products will fall and the demand for imported goods and services will increase. This reduction in international competitiveness can lead to a balance of payments **deficit**, which will in turn have a negative impact on employment levels and the rate of economic growth.

Inflation can also lead to uncertainty, which in turn reduces business activity and investment by firms. This reduction in business activity and investment is likely to have a negative impact on firms' potential for future growth and on rates of economic growth and employment in the economy.

GOVERNMENT POLICY FOR INFLATION

The main instrument used to control inflation in the UK is **monetary policy**. Monetary policy is concerned with controlling the supply of money and the cost and availability of credit.

When the Labour government came to power in 1997, one of its first actions was to hand over operational control of monetary policy to the Bank of England. The Bank of England has a 2% (+/- 1%) target for the CPI, and the MPC sets interest rates to achieve this target.

If the MPC believes that inflation is likely to go above the 2% target it will increase interest rates to dampen aggregate demand and therefore reduce inflationary pressures.

As interest rates increase, consumers will be less likely to borrow to finance spending and therefore consumption will fall. In addition, consumers with variable-rate mortgages will find that their mortgage payments will increase and therefore their **real disposable income** will fall. This fall in real disposable income will also lead to a fall in consumption.

An increase in interest rates will also cause a fall in investment by firms since borrowing to fund an investment programme becomes more expensive.

This fall in consumer spending and investment spending by firms will lead to a fall in aggregate demand in the economy, as shown in the diagram below, and will therefore lead to a fall in the price level.

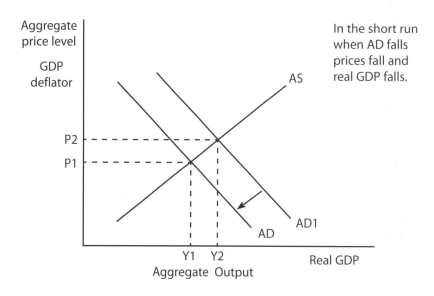

ACTIVITY 5.1

Bank hints at limited rate rises

The Bank of England has hinted that the government's inflation target of 2% may be hit more quickly than earlier thought, with only a limited interest rate rise needed.

In its quarterly inflation report, the Bank said the inflation target could be met if rates were 5.1% early next year and 5.2% later in 2007.

Analysts have been predicting a further rate rise to 5.25% from the current 5%.

The Bank also said the outlook on growth was "slightly stronger" than it had tipped in August.

The news comes a week after the Bank raised interest rates from 4.75% to 5% to try to tackle inflation, which remained at 2.4% in October.

(BBC News website, 15 November 2006)

1. Explain what is meant by the term 'inflation'.
2. Explain how inflation is measured in the UK.
3. Why does the government wish to keep inflation low and stable?
4. Explain how interest rates are used to control inflation.

Low levels of unemployment

Another one of the government's key targets is to reduce the level of unemployment in the economy.

The unemployed can be defined as "those registered able, available and willing to work at the going wage rate in any suitable job who cannot find employment".

There are two main measures of unemployment in the UK – the **Claimant Count** and the **Labour Force Survey**.

The Claimant Count

This measure of unemployment counts only people who are out of work and claiming unemployment benefits, meaning those claiming Jobseeker's Allowance (JSA).

The Claimant Count figures do not include:

- Married women with working husbands
- Those on sickness and incapacity benefit
- Those under 18 (was previously 16)
- People on training schemes

For this reason some people do not consider the Claimant Count to be an accurate measure of unemployment and therefore they prefer to use the ILO measure.

Labour Force Survey

Since 1998 the government has published an alternative measure of unemployment based on the Labour Force Survey. This measure, which is calculated by the International Labour Organization (ILO), covers those who have looked for work in the past month and are able to start work in the next two weeks.

The advantage of the Labour Force Survey is that it is an international standard and so it makes comparisons between countries much easier.

The Labour Force Survey is usually much larger (approximately 400,000 more in the UK) than the Claimant Count measure.

☐ TRENDS IN UNEMPLOYMENT

The graph opposite shows the trend in Claimant Count unemployment in Northern Ireland between 2001 and 2006. We can see that unemployment has fallen from over 6% in 2001 to about 4.7% at the end of 2006.

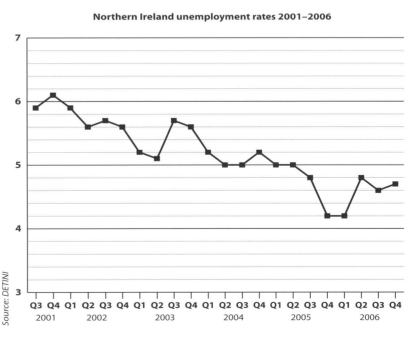

Northern Ireland unemployment rates 2001–2006

Source: DETINI

THE CAUSES OF UNEMPLOYMENT

There are many different explanations for unemployment, but the most common causes are listed below.

Demand deficient unemployment

Demand deficient or cyclical unemployment is normally associated with an **economic downturn** or a **recession**, but it may occur even when the economy is growing. It is caused by a fall in the level of aggregate demand in the economy leading to firms laying off workers in an attempt to reduce costs. In other words, there is insufficient demand in the economy for all workers to obtain employment.

Equilibrium unemployment

Sometimes unemployment exists in an economy even when aggregate demand is sufficiently high to create enough jobs for everyone who wishes to work. This type of unemployment is known as equilibrium or natural rate unemployment.

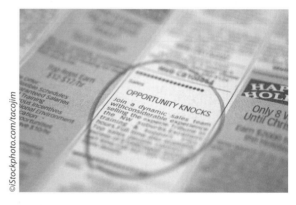
©iStockphoto.com/tacojim

This exists whenever the total number of jobs available in an economy is equal to the number of people unemployed and seeking work. For example, in the UK in 2005 just under one million people were registered as unemployed and at the same time there were over one million unfilled vacancies.

There are two main reasons why some people remain unemployed even when there are jobs available.

Frictional unemployment – this refers to job turnover in the labour market. Even when there are vacancies available it can take time to search for and find new employment and therefore workers will remain frictionally unemployed.

Structural unemployment – this exists even when there are vacancies, due to a mismatch between the skills of the unemployed and those needed by employers. For example, it would be difficult for a redundant shipyard worker from Harland and Wolff to take up employment in a high-tech computer firm.

Structural unemployment often occurs in regions due to the decline of traditional industries. For example, in the North of England the traditional coal and steel industries have declined and therefore this area has high rates of structural unemployment.

Those who are structurally unemployed are often unemployed for long periods, and the longer they remain out of work the more difficult it becomes for them to secure future employment.

WHY CONTROL UNEMPLOYMENT?

Low unemployment is obviously good for workers, but it is also good for firms since high rates of employment lead to higher levels of disposable income and therefore higher levels of consumer spending.

High levels of employment are also good for governments since more people pay income tax and the government has to pay out less money in unemployment benefit. This leaves the government with more money to put into public services such as the health service and education.

☐ GOVERNMENT POLICY FOR UNEMPLOYMENT

Recent UK government policy to reduce unemployment has focused on attempting to reduce the natural rate of unemployment through supply-side policies which will encourage individuals to take up employment by *making work pay*.

It has tried to achieve this through schemes like the following:

- It has reduced the real level of benefits and pays benefits only to those who actively seek work – JSA.
- It lowered the starting rate of income tax from 22% to 10%. In March 2007 the Chancellor of the Exchequer announced that this starting rate of 10% would be removed in April 2008 and the basic rate would be lowered to 20%.
- It created a Minimum Income Guarantee scheme for working families through the Working Families' Tax Credit, and provides help with childcare for single parents.
- If the unemployment is confined to certain regions then the approach has been to use **regional policy**. This involves the government providing start-up grants and subsidies to firms to relocate to regions with high unemployment.
- The government has also provided training to help the unemployed learn the skills necessary to gain employment.

ACTIVITY 5.2

Business is booming

Business is booming in Northern Ireland, according to the latest economic survey from the Ulster Bank.

The report said firms were enjoying high levels of customer demand and are creating new jobs as a result.

Last month, local companies reported the strongest rise in new business for more than two years.

Part of the Victoria Square development in Belfast

The report also stated that unemployment fell sharply during the past year, giving Northern Ireland an unemployment rate of 4.7%, well below the UK average of 5%.

(Adapted from Ulster Bank Economic Survey, 2006, and newspaper reports)

1. Explain the difference between the Labour Force Survey and the Claimant Count as measures of unemployment.
2. Explain one advantage and one disadvantage firms encounter as a result of lower levels of unemployment.

High but sustainable levels of economic growth

Another one of the government's macroeconomic objectives is to have high but sustainable levels of economic growth.

Economic growth occurs whenever the total output of an economy increases. In other words, it is when there is an increase in the real level of national income and is measured by the percentage change in real **Gross Domestic Product (GDP)** or **Gross National Product (GNP)**. GDP is defined as the total value of all output produced within the domestic boundaries of a country in any given year.

To obtain a figure for economic growth the government calculates the percentage change in GDP from one year to the next.

TRENDS IN ECONOMIC GROWTH

In the past, growth rates have tended to fluctuate quite significantly around the average or trend growth rate. Periods of high growth were normally followed by periods of low or even negative growth. This pattern of growth is known as the **economic cycle** and is illustrated in the diagram below.

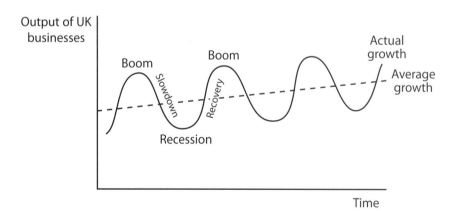

A **boom** occurs when an economy experiences rates of growth which are well above the trend rate. The UK economy experienced a boom between 1986 and 1988, and 1997 and 1998.

A **recession** occurs when an economy experiences negative growth rates for two consecutive quarters (ie six months). The last recession experienced by the UK economy was 1990 to 1992.

A **slowdown** occurs when growth rates are falling but are not yet negative. The UK economy experienced a slowdown between 1998 and 2000.

A **recovery** occurs when growth rates increase after a recession or a slowdown. For example, the UK experienced a recovery between 1992 and 1994, and again after the slowdown caused by the terrorist attacks on 11 September 2001.

The government today tries to keep growth rates steady at around 2% to 3%. It regards this as being sustainable – that is, an acceptable growth rate which will not lead to inflation.

Gordon Brown, during his time as Chancellor, claimed that *prudent* management of the economy would lead to an end to the **boom/bust cycle** as shown opposite and that the economy could grow constantly at the sustainable (trend) rate.

The UK economic cycle – growth rate of real GDP

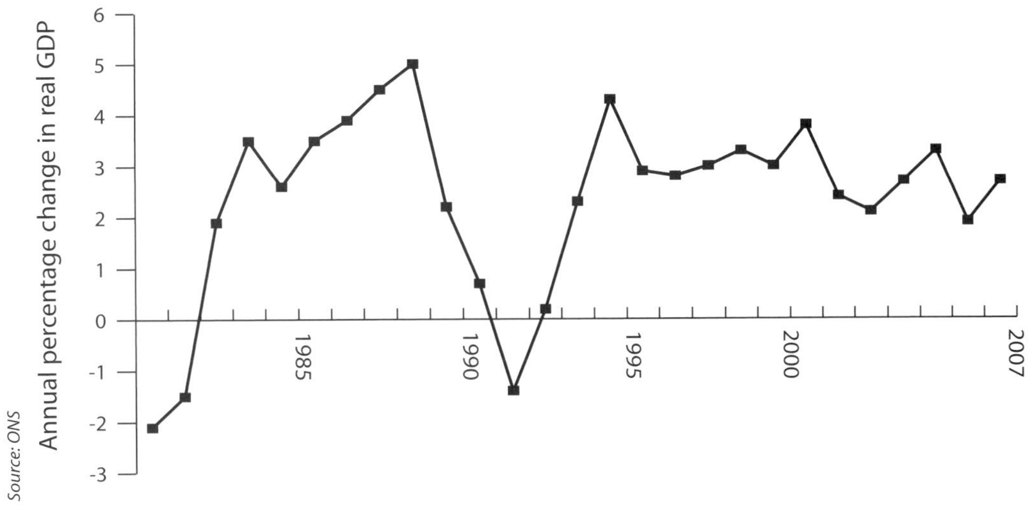

Source: ONS

WHY AIM FOR ECONOMIC GROWTH?

There are a number of benefits associated with higher rates of economic growth, including the following.

Higher levels of employment

Evidence suggests that there is an inverse relationship between the level of unemployment and the rate of economic growth.

This relationship exists because as the economy grows more people will be needed to produce the increased output and therefore employment levels will increase.

Increased government revenue

The second advantage of economic growth is that it leads to higher levels of tax revenue for the government. As an economy grows and incomes and employment rates rise, the revenue that the government receives from taxation will increase without it having to increase tax rates. This extra revenue can be spent on improving the economy.

The impressive growth rates of the UK throughout the 1990s left the Chancellor with a large budget **surplus**, which was used for increases in education and health spending. However, the more recent economic slowdown has reduced tax receipts and left the government facing a growing budget deficit.

Increased investment

Economic data suggests that as economic growth rates increase the level of investment undertaken by firms also increases. The increasing output and demand associated with high rates of growth will encourage further investment by firms, which will in turn lead to even more growth in the future.

DISADVANTAGES OF ECONOMIC GROWTH

While high rates of economic growth are beneficial to an economy in many ways, it should be remembered that they can also bring some problems. These disadvantages of economic growth include the following.

Inflation

If the economy grows too quickly then aggregate demand will increase faster than aggregate supply. This could then lead to higher rates of inflation.

Pollution

When an economy grows it uses up more resources to produce the higher levels of output required to satisfy demand. By using more resources the economy is likely to create more waste and cause greater levels of pollution.

It is because of these disadvantages of economic growth that the government has qualified its objective by claiming it wishes to achieve high *but sustainable* levels of economic growth. Sustainable economic growth occurs whenever the economy enjoys a high level of growth but this growth does not cause large increases in inflation or pollution.

GOVERNMENT POLICY FOR ECONOMIC GROWTH

Economic growth takes place whenever there is an increase in either the *quantity* or *quality* of resources available to an economy.

Economies grow when the quantity of resources available increases. For example, the UK grew strongly in the past because of the discovery of North Sea oil, and Saudi Arabia has grown because it has exploited its oil reserves.

An increase in the quality of resources also leads to growth. Investing in education and training will increase the value of **human capital** which makes workers more productive. Investing in new machinery and equipment will also lead to increased productivity and therefore economic growth.

Current government policy for achieving high but sustainable levels of economic growth has focused on trying to improve the quality of resources available in the economy. It has tried to achieve this through supply-side measures such as:

- Making changes to the education system to include more vocational education
- Making grants and subsidies available to entrepreneurs to help them start and grow their business
- Providing training schemes for the unemployed, such as the New Deal programme, to help them back into work
- Creating a tax and benefit system which encourages enterprise and hard work

The government can also achieve higher levels of economic growth (in the short run at least) through policies which are designed to increase the level of aggregate demand in the economy.

For example, if the government was to cut the basic rate of income tax this would result in an increase in real disposable income which in turn should lead to higher levels of consumer spending. An increase in consumer spending causes aggregate demand to increase which in turn causes firms to increase output to meet this extra demand, and therefore the economy grows as a result.

The diagram below shows how an increase in aggregate demand can lead to an increase in real GDP and therefore economic growth.

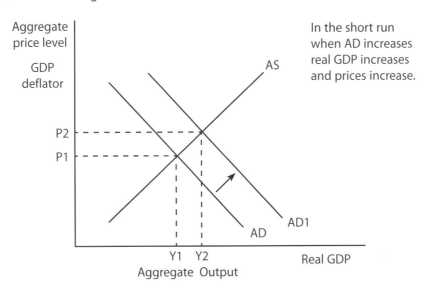

The problem with trying to increase economic growth through increases in aggregate demand is that this can lead to higher levels of inflation, as the diagram illustrates.

ACTIVITY 5.3

Interest rate cut expected as growth slows

The likelihood of interest rate cuts rose sharply yesterday after new figures showed growth falling to its lowest level in two years. The weak 0.3% expansion in the final three months of the year pulled the annual growth rate of real GDP down to 1.8%.

Economists had expected growth to fall, but the scale of the decline took them by surprise. The Office for National Statistics (ONS) said output in business services was particularly weak.

A spokesman for the Confederation of British Industry (CBI) claimed that "these figures, together with fears of a global slowdown next year, may well remove the final obstacle to the MPC cutting interest rates".

(Adapted from www.scotsman.com, July 2005)

1. Explain what is meant by the term 'economic growth'.
2. The first paragraph states that growth fell to 1.8%. Does this mean that the UK economy was experiencing a recession? Explain your answer.
3. Explain why lower growth rates might lead to the MPC cutting interest rates.

An acceptable balance of payments

The government's fourth key macroeconomic objective is to achieve an acceptable position on the balance of payments.

The balance of payments is a set of national accounts which measures the net flow of exports and imports into and out of a country over a given time period.

The UK balance of payments account is divided into three sections:

- The current account
- The capital account
- The financial account

The current account measures the export and import of goods and services into and out of the UK. The capital and financial accounts measure the flow of money involved in the purchase and sale of external assets and liabilities. External assets are items of value situated abroad but owned by UK residents, for example homes, pubs, bank accounts, and bonds purchased in other countries. An external liability is an item of value situated in the UK but owned by a foreign resident.

©iStockphoto.com/duncan1890

The current account is the most important part of the UK balance of payments. A current account deficit means the UK imports more goods and services than it exports. A current account surplus means that the UK exports more goods and services than it imports.

☐ TRENDS IN THE BALANCE OF PAYMENTS

The chart opposite shows the UK current account balance over the last six years. We can see that the UK has been experiencing a consistent current account deficit.

☐ WHY TARGET THE BALANCE OF PAYMENTS?

The government's objective is to try and achieve an acceptable position on the balance of payments. However, there is some debate within economics over how much importance should be placed on the balance of payments accounts, and over what constitutes an acceptable balance of payments.

The UK currently has a very large deficit on the current account of the balance of payments. Some economists see this as a sign of economic weakness and are therefore concerned with trying to correct the deficit. They argue that a current account deficit means there is a net outflow of money leaving the UK economy to pay for foreign products, and that this will in turn lead to lower levels of employment and growth.

Other economists do not see the deficit on the current account as being a major problem. This is because the UK has a large surplus on the capital and financial accounts which offsets the current account deficit. Current government policy seems to side with this view, with the balance of payments not being very high up on the government's list of concerns.

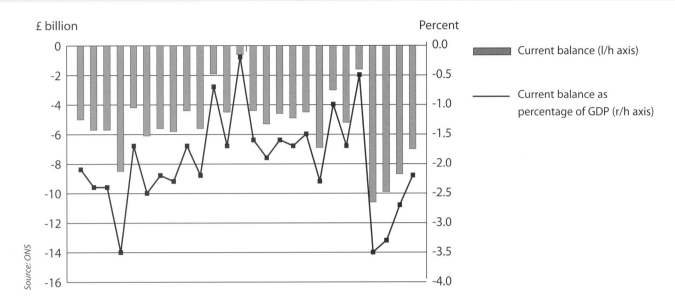

Source: ONS

GOVERNMENT POLICY FOR THE BALANCE OF PAYMENTS

As stated earlier, the UK government is not very concerned with the current account deficit, but if it was concerned it could use the following strategies to correct the deficit.

Devalue or depreciate the exchange rate

A devaluation of the exchange rate will increase the price of imports relative to exports. Domestic demand for home-produced goods will increase and the demand for exports should also increase since they have fallen in price. This should then help to cure the balance of payments deficit.

However, the effectiveness of devaluation in reducing a deficit will depend on the PED for exports and imports.

Introduce tariffs or import controls

The second method a government could use to reduce a current account deficit would be to introduce some type of trade barrier to reduce imports. Examples of import controls include tariffs, quotas and exchange controls. However, membership of the World Trade Organization (WTO) and the EU makes using these import controls difficult.

Government policy instruments

We have learnt about the four key macroeconomic objectives the government has set itself in order to create a healthy economy. There are a number of policy instruments which can be used to help achieve these objectives.

These policy instruments include monetary policy, fiscal policy, regional policy, and supply-side policies.

MONETARY POLICY

Monetary policy is concerned with controlling the supply of money in the economy and controlling the cost and availability of credit.

Monetary policy in the UK is used almost entirely to achieve the government's target for inflation.

It is controlled by the MPC at the Bank of England and involves changes to the rate of interest which the Bank of England charges to the retail banks borrowing money from it.

As stated earlier, the Bank of England has a 2% (+/- 1%) target for the CPI and the MPC sets interest rates to achieve this target. If the MPC believes that inflation is likely to go above the 2% target, it will increase interest rates to dampen aggregate demand and therefore reduce inflationary pressures. When the Bank of England changes the rate it charges, the retail banks will also change the rate they charge their customers.

As interest rates in the economy increase, consumers will be less likely to borrow to finance spending and therefore consumption will fall. In addition, consumers with mortgages will find that their mortgage payments will increase and so their real disposable income will fall. This fall in real disposable income will also lead to a fall in consumption.

An increase in interest rates will also cause a fall in investment by firms since borrowing to fund an investment programme becomes more expensive.

This fall in consumer spending and investment spending by firms will lead to a fall in total demand in the economy and thus a fall in the price level.

FISCAL POLICY

Fiscal policy is the use of government spending, taxation and borrowing to influence the level of aggregate demand in the economy. The government can try to influence this level through directly altering tax rates and the amount it spends on services.

If unemployment in the economy is high the government can increase its spending and reduce taxation to increase aggregate demand in the economy and therefore decrease unemployment. This decrease in taxes and the increase in government spending will give consumers more disposable income. They will then spend this extra money, thereby increasing aggregate demand in the economy which in turn leads to an increase in employment and economic growth.

The budget

Each year in the budget the Chancellor sets out the government's fiscal policy plans for the forthcoming year. The Chancellor explains in the budget how much revenue the government expects to receive from taxation and how this revenue will be spent.

The charts below and opposite show the main sources of government revenue and the main areas where this tax revenue is spent.

Where taxes come from

Total receipts – £487 billion

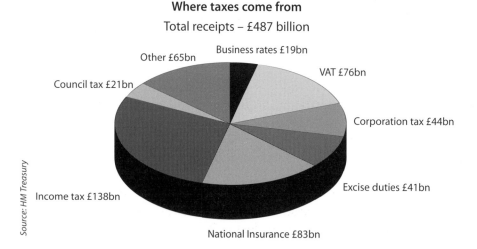

Business rates £19bn
Other £65bn
VAT £76bn
Council tax £21bn
Corporation tax £44bn
Excise duties £41bn
Income tax £138bn
National Insurance £83bn

Source: HM Treasury

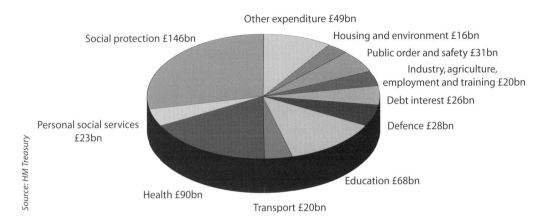

Where taxpayers' money is spent

Total managed expenditure – £519 billion

Other expenditure £49bn

Social protection £146bn

Housing and environment £16bn

Public order and safety £31bn

Industry, agriculture, employment and training £20bn

Debt interest £26bn

Defence £28bn

Personal social services £23bn

Education £68bn

Health £90bn

Transport £20bn

Source: HM Treasury

The first chart shows how much money the government expected to raise from the various taxes between April 2006 and April 2007. We can see that the government estimated that total tax revenue from all sources would be £487 billion.

We can also see from the second chart that total public spending was estimated to be around £519 billion in the same year. That is around £8,700 for every man, woman and child in the UK. This figure is set to rise to £549 billion in 2007 to 2008, and to £580 billion in 2008 to 2009.

This means that the Chancellor had planned to borrow £32 billion over the course of the 2006 to 2007 financial year.

When government revenue exceeds government spending it is known as a budget surplus, whereas when spending exceeds revenue it is known as a budget deficit.

Taxation

Taxation can be defined as the compulsory transfer of money from a private individual or organisation to local or central government.

Governments impose tax on households and business organisations for a number of reasons:

- The first reason is to correct market failures. Market failure occurs whenever the market mechanism leads to an outcome which is inefficient or which is not satisfactory from the point of view of society. Examples of market failures include pollution and congestion.

  We saw earlier in this chapter how taxes can be used to reduce pollution levels in the economy. Examples of environmental taxes include the Climate Change Levy and the landfill tax.

- Taxes are also levied to raise money which can be used to pay for government expenditure. The chart above illustrates the amount of revenue required by the government to enable it to provide public services like the National Health Service (NHS) and the education system.

- Taxation can be used to manage the economy as a whole. We learned in this chapter how taxes can be used to influence the level of aggregate demand, and therefore the levels of growth and employment in the economy.

- Taxes are also used to redistribute income from the rich to the poor. Those who earn higher incomes generally pay more tax than those on lower incomes, and some of this tax revenue is used to fund social security benefits for the less well off.

One way to classify a tax is to consider the way it is levied.

Direct taxes – these are taxes which are levied directly on an individual or organisation. These include taxes such as income tax, National Insurance Contributions and corporation tax.

Indirect taxes – these, on the other hand, are taxes which are levied on goods or services. An indirect tax is a tax on expenditure and this includes taxes such as VAT and excise duty.

Another way to classify a tax is to consider the incidence or 'burden' of the tax as a proportion of income.

Progressive tax – this is where the proportion of income paid in tax increases as income increases. An example of a progressive tax is income tax because as your income increases you pay a higher proportion of that income in tax. Income tax in the UK has three bands – the basic rate at 10%, the starting rate at 20% and the higher rate at 40%. However, as stated earlier, in March 2007 the Chancellor announced that this starting rate of 10% would be removed in April 2008 and the basic rate would be lowered to 20%.

The chart below is an example of how progressive income tax is. We can see that as income increases the proportion of income paid in tax increases. Those earning less than £5,000 pay 1% of their income in tax, whereas those on over £100,000 pay 33% income tax.

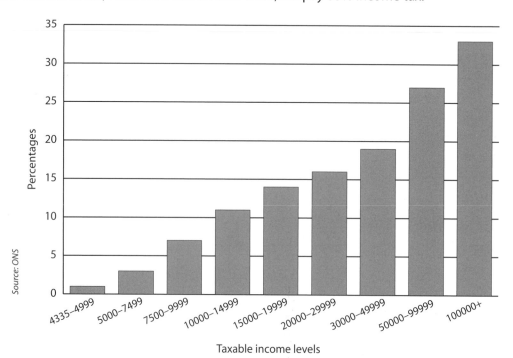

Source: ONS

Taxable income levels

Regressive tax – this is where the proportion of income paid in tax decreases as income increases. A regressive tax therefore hits the poorest in society hardest. For example, the fee associated with the television licence is a regressive tax since everyone pays the same amount, but this amount represents a higher proportion of a poor person's income. Most indirect taxes, like excise duties on cigarettes and alcohol, are regressive. The chart opposite shows the duty on tobacco as a percentage of disposable income.

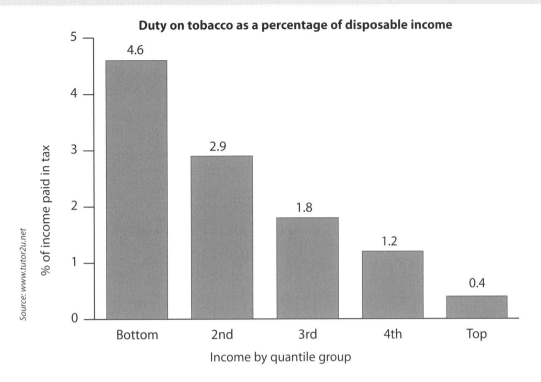

Duty on tobacco as a percentage of disposable income

Source: www.tutor2u.net

% of income paid in tax — Income by quantile group

Bottom: 4.6 | 2nd: 2.9 | 3rd: 1.8 | 4th: 1.2 | Top: 0.4

Proportional tax – this is where the proportion of income paid in tax stays the same as income increases. Proportional taxes are not very common in advanced economies. National Insurance, which is 11% for every employee who earns over a certain income, is the best example of a UK tax which is broadly proportional.

Benefits, subsidies and grants

Benefits, subsidies and grants can be dealt with together because they all have similar effects on the economy.

Benefits – these are payments made to individuals who are out of work, who have a disability or whose incomes are below a certain level.

Welfare benefits include JSA, Disability Living Allowance (DLA) and Income Support. These benefits redistribute income from the relatively better off to those on lower incomes.

If we look again at the chart on government expenditure on page 75, we can see that the payment of benefits for social protection accounts for the greatest proportion of government expenditure, with over £146 billion being spent in this area each year.

Subsidies – a subsidy is a form of government assistance, generally a **grant**, which is given to firms to help them in the production of a particular good or service.

Subsidies do not always entail the payment of grants. They can also refer to the tax exemptions and reductions that a firm may receive, either through tax breaks or the accelerated depreciation scheme.

As we learned in Chapter 2, these subsidies reduce the costs of production and therefore allow firms to produce higher levels of output at lower prices.

REGIONAL POLICY

In the UK not all regions enjoy the same economic and social conditions and so there are regional disparities in income and employment levels. In Northern Ireland for example, GDP per head is still substantially below the UK average and economic inactivity rates are among the highest in the UK.

The aim of regional policy is to redistribute funds from the high-performing parts of the UK to the poorly-performing regions. Regional policy is administered through regional development agencies such as Invest Northern Ireland, and generally entails the provision of investment grants for firms in Assisted Areas.

There is some debate among economists over the benefit of regional assistance, with some arguing that it simply subsidises inefficient firms which would not survive without government help. This view is reflected in current government policy, with a decreasing proportion of government spending being given over to regional policy assistance in recent years.

SUPPLY-SIDE POLICIES

In recent years the government has focused on using other policies to control inflation and unemployment. These are known as supply-side policies and include policies such as grants to small businesses and education reforms.

The aim of supply-side policies is to shift the aggregate supply curve to the right, allowing the economy to enjoy higher levels of employment and economic growth without any increase in the inflation rate.

Examples of supply-side policies include income tax cuts, education and training reforms, support to businesses, and labour market policies.

Income tax cuts

Economists who support supply-side policies believe that lower rates of income tax give people an incentive to work longer hours or take a new job because they get to keep a higher percentage of the money they earn.

In the past the government focused income tax cuts on those with higher incomes, but in recent years attention has shifted to lower-income households. In the late 1990s, a new lower starting rate of tax of 10% was introduced by the Labour government, and the band of income on which this was paid was later widened. As stated earlier, in March 2007 the Chancellor announced that this starting rate of 10% would be removed in April 2008 and the basic rate would be lowered to 20%.

Cutting tax rates for lower-paid workers should help to reduce the extent of the "unemployment trap" – where people calculate that they may be no better off from working than if they stay outside the labour force – and therefore help to reduce unemployment.

Education and training reforms

The current government is constantly adapting the education and training system in an attempt to improve the quality of human capital. For example, there is now a greater focus on vocational qualifications and retraining schemes for the unemployed. Schemes like the New Deal have also been designed to help get the unemployed back into work.

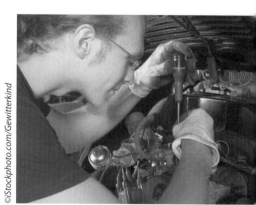

©iStockphoto.com/Gewitterkind

Support to businesses

Firms in certain areas are given grants and assistance to help them develop and grow. The unemployed are also offered grants to help them start their own businesses. The objective with these schemes is to increase enterprise.

©iStockphoto.com/Typogigo

Supply-side policies also include tax relief on research and development and reductions in the rate of corporation tax. The Republic of Ireland is a good example of an EU country that has benefited hugely from cutting company taxes. The 12.5% corporation tax rate effective in the Republic of Ireland has led to a large rise in foreign direct investment, which in turn has helped to fuel the high rates of economic growth experienced in the Republic.

Labour market policies

The introduction of the Welfare to Work programmes, such as the New Deal and the Working Families' Tax Credits, aims to encourage the unemployed to take up employment. The recent changes to the JSA agreements (people now have to sign on every week and must be willing to travel up to one and a half hours to work) make it more difficult for people to claim benefits.

POLICY TRADE-OFFS

There is a major problem for governments in attempting to achieve a healthy economy in that, when they use a policy to try and achieve one economic objective, it may actually cause problems elsewhere.

For example, if the Bank of England increases interest rates in an attempt to achieve low inflation this may lead to a decrease in aggregate demand and therefore cause an increase in unemployment and a reduction in economic growth. An increase in interest rates may also cause the exchange rate to increase, having a negative effect on exporters.

Equally, if the government tries to increase economic growth by loosening fiscal policy it may lead to increases in aggregate demand and cause demand-pull inflation.

It is these trade-offs which make it very difficult for the government to successfully manage the economy. Trying to improve one area of the economy to help one group or achieve one objective can upset other groups or cause problems for the other objectives.

For this reason, the government has increasingly moved towards using supply-side policies rather than demand-side policies as a means of managing the economy. This is because it believes the trade-offs associated with supply-side policies are much less than those associated with policies designed to increase aggregate demand.

The more frequent use of these supply-side policies has certainly increased the enterprise culture and led to a more flexible labour market, and so can be described as being relatively successful. This success is clearly illustrated by the fact that inflation and unemployment in the UK are at historically low levels while the economy has continued to grow quite strongly.

However, supply-side policies are not the only policies which should be used. To be truly effective in meeting its four key objectives, the government needs to use supply-side policies *in conjunction* with the other policies such as monetary policy and fiscal policy.

REVISION QUESTIONS

1. Explain three advantages and three disadvantages of high levels of competition.
2. Using examples, explain three reasons why governments intervene in markets.
3. What is meant by the term 'inflation'?
4. Explain how the government attempts to control inflation.
5. Explain two causes of inflation.
6. Explain some of the policies the government uses to control unemployment.
7. What is meant by economic growth?
8. Explain the difference between an economic slowdown and an economic recession.
9. Why are very high rates of growth considered to be undesirable?
10. Explain what is measured in the balance of payments accounts.
11. Explain how the government could correct a current account deficit.
12. What is meant by the term 'fiscal policy'?
13. Distinguish between direct and indirect taxation.
14. Distinguish between progressive and regressive taxation.
15. Explain, with examples, the term 'supply-side policies'.

CASE STUDY

Changing shopping habits lift value market to £7.8 billion
(Adapted from the BBC News website, 21 July 2006, and the _Telegraph_ website, 31 October 2006)

Shoppers' love affair with discount clothing retailers like Primark continues unabated, with Verdict Research predicting that nearly £1 of every £4 spent on clothing this year will be with a value retailer.

The growth of retailers like Primark and supermarket clothing brands over the last decade has fundamentally changed the way people shop for clothes.

Maureen Hinton, senior analyst at Verdict Research, said "Not only have discount retailers been the main drivers of price deflation in the market – in the process causing a fundamental price shift across the whole market – they have also been almost entirely responsible for any new growth over the past two years."

The value market is now worth £7.8 billion, says Verdict Research in its latest report – UK Value Clothing Retailers 2006. In 2001, the value sector accounted for 16% of the overall clothing market; today it is almost a quarter.

Market share of value retailers

Market share (%)	2005	2006
George at Asda	17.8	17.3
Primark	12.9	15.7
New Look	10.7	11.4
Tesco	10.3	11
Matalan	11.8	10.7

Source: Competition Commission

However, Verdict warns that not every discount retailer is benefiting from the boom. Mrs Hinton said "Not all value retailers are prospering. More than 90% of their growth this year will come from four operators: Primark, New Look, Tesco and George, and of these, Primark accounts for the lion's share at 42.8% ... With clothing market growth at its lowest since the turn of the millennium, and operating costs rising, smaller operators are struggling as larger players intensify the competition with aggressive space growth. Both smaller operators and new entrants have little opportunity to build the scale necessary to run a profitable price-led proposition. The value model relies on scale, cost efficiencies and high footfall to support its low price position and high volume sales."

Not everyone is happy with the growth in the value clothing market. People have asked if the Northern Ireland shopper is paying £2 for a T-shirt, how much is the person who's making it being paid? Safia Minney of People Tree commented, "We can use fashion as a development tool to help people escape from poverty."

Many high street stores – including Primark and Peacocks – now belong to the Ethical Trading Initiative (ETI), which makes sure they adhere to a code of conduct covering working conditions, wages and the right to belong to a union.

However, unless clothes are advertised as ethical there is no way of knowing how they were made. This has led to growing calls for a label which would show fashion lovers they can hand over their few pounds for the latest fashion and still have a clear conscience.

Using the information on the previous page, answer the questions below.

1. Use the information in the first and fourth paragraphs to calculate the approximate value of the UK clothing market.

2. Use the information in the table to determine which retailer has experienced the greatest growth and the greatest fall in market share between 2005 and 2006.

3. Explain why small operators and new entrants are finding it difficult to compete in this sector of the clothing market.

4. What is meant by the term 'deflation', as used in the third paragraph?

5. How might intense price competition in the UK clothing market impact upon wages and working conditions in the factories which produce the clothes?

6. Explain how ethical labelling might alleviate these problems.

7. Examine three types of non-price competition used by clothes retailers in Northern Ireland.

CHAPTER 6

International competition

In Chapter 3 we learned how the level of competition in the domestic market would influence the conduct and behaviour of the firms operating within that market.

In this chapter we will look at the international dimension of competition and will study the impact globalisation and international competition has had on businesses in Northern Ireland.

International trade

This refers to the exchange of goods and services across international boundaries.

Since the mid 1980s businesses in Northern Ireland have increasingly looked beyond the local and national markets in Northern Ireland and the rest of the UK, and have begun to look more closely at competing in markets in other countries. Exports from Northern Ireland's manufacturing sector now account for over 30% of all manufacturing sales and are worth over £4 billion to the Northern Ireland economy.

There are a number of reasons why firms in Northern Ireland are keen to trade on an international basis. They include the following.

☐ TO GAIN ACCESS TO LARGER MARKETS

One of the most obvious reasons for trading internationally is that it allows firms to increase the size of their potential market. A Northern Ireland firm which decides to sell its products in the EU, as opposed to just Northern Ireland, will increase its number of potential customers from 1.9 million to over 500 million.

☐ TO GAIN ECONOMIES OF SCALE

If firms produce on a larger scale in order to meet the demands of the increased market, they should be able to avail of economies of scale. As we saw in Chapter 4, economies of scale are the advantages of increased size that lead to falling average costs. If a firm can gain these economies of scale it will become more competitive and, as a result, more profitable.

☐ DIVERSIFICATION

Another reason why firms trade internationally is to diversify and therefore reduce the risk of sudden changes in demand. If a firm operates only in its domestic market then its performance will be closely linked to the performance of that economy – if the economy experiences a recession then the firm's sales will fall as a result. However, if a firm operates in a number of markets then it will be able to rely on its sales to other countries if it finds that sales to one country are falling.

SATURATED HOME MARKET

Another reason why firms may expand overseas is because their home market has become saturated. For example, the market for washing machines in Northern Ireland could be considered to be saturated since the **diffusion rate** (the proportion of the population owning a product) is over 90%. In India, on the other hand, the diffusion rate for washing machines is less than 40% and so India represents a much more attractive market for the makers of washing machines.

PRESSURE FROM SHAREHOLDERS

A final reason which might explain why Northern Ireland firms are very keen to trade globally is that they may be under pressure from their shareholders to increase profit levels. As we saw in Chapter 4, shareholders will often want profits to increase year after year, and in some cases the only way for a firm to ensure its profits increase is to attempt selling its products in new markets overseas.

The pattern of Northern Ireland trade

Northern Ireland is a region of the UK and so imports and exports to and from Northern Ireland will be recorded as UK trade.

It is therefore very difficult to get precise figures for imports and exports into and out of Northern Ireland. The problem is particularly acute when trying to measure the value of imports into Northern Ireland, since some of the goods may have been imported to other parts of the UK first and then shipped to Northern Ireland. If this is the case, then the goods would be recorded as internal trade rather than as imports.

Despite these problems, the government does try to collect figures on the value and destination of Northern Ireland exports.

Belfast docks

Destination of Northern Ireland exports

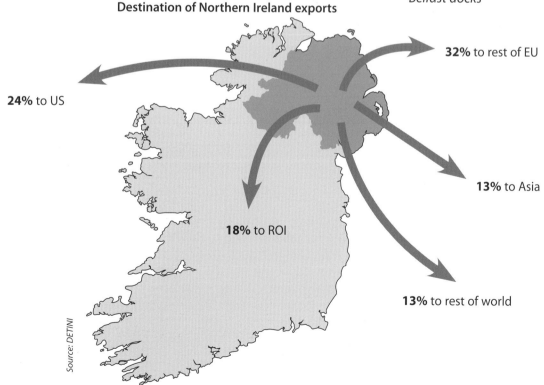

32% to rest of EU

24% to US

13% to Asia

18% to ROI

13% to rest of world

Source: DETINI

ACTIVITY 6.1

Northern Ireland manufacturing exports on the rise

Total sales and exports reported by manufacturing companies in Northern Ireland have continued to increase over the last year.

The value of exports has risen by 3.5% over the year and now represents almost a third of all manufacturing sales. The Republic of Ireland is Northern Ireland's single most important export market for manufactured goods, with exports continuing to rise – this year by 11.6% – to stand at an estimated £1.2 billion.

Sales outside the EU were worth £2.1 billion in 2004 to 2005, with sales to China estimated to be worth some 5% of this market.

Commenting on the figures, Enterprise Minister Angela Smith said "It is encouraging to see the rise in Northern Ireland's manufacturing sales and exports. Northern Ireland's manufacturers must continue to explore new markets and take full advantage of the opportunities that are presented by those areas of the world, such as China, which are experiencing high levels of growth."

(Northern Ireland Manufacturing Sales and Exports Survey,
Department of Enterprise, Trade and Investment – DETINI, October 2006)

1. Explain the difference between a Northern Ireland export and a Northern Ireland import.
2. The second paragraph states that "The Republic of Ireland is Northern Ireland's single most important export market for manufactured goods". Explain some of the possible reasons why this might be the case.
3. Why would high levels of growth in China make it an attractive market for Northern Ireland exporters?

The benefits of international trade

Economists argue that there are great benefits to be gained by everyone if countries open themselves up to international trade. A number of arguments are put forward to support free trade, including the following.

☐ INCREASED GROWTH THROUGH COMPARATIVE ADVANTAGE

The strongly-held conviction about the benefits of international trade is based on the work of a nineteenth-century economist called David Ricardo. Ricardo devised an economic model which he called "the theory of comparative advantage".

Through this model Ricardo was able to demonstrate how countries could increase their output and GDP through specialising in the production of those goods where they had a comparative advantage, and trading freely with others who had also specialised according to their comparative advantage.

☐ INCREASED COMPETITION

The second benefit of international trade is that it leads to an increase in competition. As we learned in Chapter 3, this increase in competition from foreign producers will lead to a reduction in monopoly power and will therefore lead to lower prices, higher quality goods and services, and increased efficiency.

☐ IMPORT OF NEW IDEAS AND TECHNOLOGY

International trade can also lead to the sharing of ideas and technology between firms which will have a positive impact on all firms. For example, in the UK many manufacturing firms have benefited from adopting the lean production ideas of the Japanese.

☐ INCREASED EMPLOYMENT

We have already learned how an increase in international trade can lead to an increase in GDP through the principle of comparative advantage. This increase in economic growth will in turn also lead to an increase in employment, since aggregate demand in the economy will be higher.

The case for restricting international trade

In spite of the many advantages of international trade, countries do sometimes impose restrictions or barriers on imports from other countries.

They do this for a number of reasons.

☐ TO PROTECT DOMESTIC JOBS FROM FOREIGN COMPETITION

One of the most common arguments in favour of import restrictions is that they help to protect domestic firms from foreign competition, resulting in the protection of domestic jobs.

☐ TO PROTECT INFANT INDUSTRIES

Another argument used to justify import restrictions is that they protect young industries and allow them the time to develop free from competition. Once these infant industries have grown and developed they will be better prepared to face competition. The import barriers can then be removed.

☐ TO PROTECT SENILE/DECLINING INDUSTRIES

Restrictions can also be helpful to declining industries such as steel and coal, allowing them to restructure their operations and adjust to the increased levels of foreign competition. This argument has been used in the US to justify the 30% tariffs imposed on imported steel.

☐ TO PROTECT STRATEGIC INDUSTRIES

Some industries, such as agriculture and armaments, are regarded as strategic industries which are important in times of war. Traditionally, these industries have been protected from foreign competition.

©iStockphoto.com/myrrha

☐ TO GAIN REVENUE

Import taxes can also be used to raise revenue for the government. These taxes (or tariffs) are popular with governments and voters since the tax burden appears to fall upon foreign firms.

Trade barriers

The term 'trade barrier' refers to any form of government intervention which has the effect of reducing international trade. Trade barriers can take many forms and include the following.

☐ TARIFFS

A tariff is an indirect tax which is levied upon imported goods and services. It is also known as an import duty or a customs duty.

Imposing a tariff on imports will raise their price relative to that of domestically-produced goods and will therefore make home-produced goods more competitive. The added bonus of a tariff is that it also raises revenue for the government.

☐ QUOTAS

A quota is a physical limit on the quantity of a good that can be imported into a country. Imposing a quota on a particular product will lead to an increase in the share of the market available to domestic producers. In 2006 the EU, in response to complaints from Spanish and French textile producers, introduced quotas on the import of textiles from China.

☐ ADMINISTRATION REGULATIONS

Some countries require importers to complete numerous documents before an import licence is awarded. In addition, countries often refuse to import certain products on the grounds that they are unsafe or produced in a way which harms the environment. For example, the EU has banned the import of American beef due to concerns about the use of growth hormones.

While there may be legitimate reasons for using these regulations, they have the effect of reducing imports and therefore can be considered to be trade barriers.

☐ DOMESTIC SUBSIDIES

A subsidy is a form of government assistance, generally a grant, or increasingly a tax exemption, which is given to firms to help them in the production of a particular good or service. These subsidies allow domestic firms to produce higher levels of output at more competitive prices and therefore lead to a reduction in imports.

☐ VOLUNTARY AGREEMENTS

In order to avoid the damaging consequences of a trade war, countries do sometimes reach agreements about the level of trade conducted between them.

In some cases a nation's government can agree to restrict the level of goods it exports to its trading partner. With a Voluntary Export Restriction (VER) the exporting country sets an absolute limit on the number of goods it will sell to its trading partner. The government then sells an export licence to domestic firms to export up to the agreed limit.

Although these agreements are called 'voluntary' they are rarely completely voluntary since they are generally imposed upon the insistence of the importing nation.

☐ FOREIGN EXCHANGE CONTROLS

In some cases governments place restrictions on the amount of foreign or local currency that can be traded or purchased. If a government does this then it can indirectly limit the value of goods that can be imported. This is because a firm will require foreign currency in order to import goods.

Today these exchange controls are used only by weaker transitional economies, or what the International Monetary Fund (IMF) calls "Article 14" countries. Examples include Argentina and Brazil. Exchange controls have not been used in the UK since 1979.

ACTIVITY 6.2

Brussels extends Asia shoe tariff

Imports of leather shoes from China and Vietnam to Europe will continue to face steep punitive tariffs, under a deal recently reached by EU governments.

In future, imports from China will face tariffs of 16.5%, and imports from Vietnam will face a 10% levy.

The agreement was welcomed in Italy, where government ministers have claimed that unfair competition from manufacturers in both countries is driving its own shoe producers out of business.

However, the duties were opposed by a large number of member states – including Germany, Sweden and the UK – which saw them as an unwelcome barrier to trade.

Retailers in the EU have responded angrily, and claim that EU consumers will end up paying more for their footwear.

(Adapted from BBC News website, 4 October 2006)

1. Explain what is meant by the term 'trade barrier'.
2. Explain how the imposition of a tariff on imported shoes will make shoes produced in the EU more competitive.
3. Consider three alternative trade barriers that could be used to restrict the import of shoes from China.

Globalisation

Trying to define globalisation precisely is a very difficult process. Over the last ten years hundreds of books and thousands of articles have been written on the topic, and in each of these books and articles globalisation has been defined differently.

Globalisation has many features. Some of these are social – for example, the spread of American or Western culture, which is sometimes referred to as Americanisation – and some are political, for example increased immigration and the increasing power of quasi-governmental organisations like the WTO.

From an economic or business perspective, globalisation refers to the development of powerful global brands and the development of multinational businesses which source their materials and components on a worldwide basis.

Some people feel that a definition of globalisation should incorporate all of these social, political and economic aspects. However, from a purely business perspective globalisation can be defined as "the term used to describe the way in which markets across the world are becoming increasingly integrated".

☐ CAUSES OF GLOBALISATION

There are a number of reasons why firms now find it easier to operate on a global scale, including the following.

Developments in ICT

The vast improvements in communications brought about by developments in Information and Communications Technology (ICT) over the last 25 years mean than firms now find it much easier to communicate and handle data on a global basis.

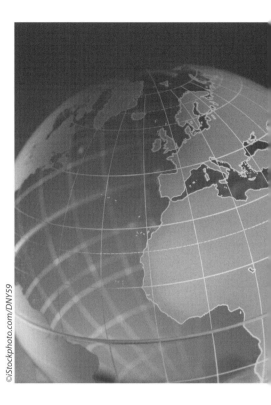

©iStockphoto.com/DNY59

Reduction in transport costs

Technological improvements coupled with greater competition in air and to a lesser extent sea freight, has significantly reduced the cost involved in transporting goods. This reduction in transport costs has meant that it is now cheaper to produce goods in low-wage countries and deliver them to markets around the world.

Reduction in trade barriers

Over the last 50 years there has been a marked reduction in trade barriers such as tariffs and quotas, mainly as a result of the work of the WTO. This has made it much easier for firms to operate on a global scale.

Reduction in international capital restrictions

The reduction in exchange controls and international capital restrictions since 1979 has meant that business capital can move freely from one country to another. This has made it much easier for businesses to invest in other countries.

Business strategies to deal with internationalisation

The **deregulation** of international trade has meant that Northern Ireland firms now face much greater levels of competition from foreign firms which may have significant advantages in terms of costs, expertise or spending power.

On the other hand, the trend towards free trade and globalisation also presents Northern Ireland firms with the opportunity to expand their operations into new markets.

If Northern Ireland firms are to survive in this environment it is crucial that they maximise the opportunities presented to them by globalisation, while at the same time taking whatever action is necessary to minimise the potential threats posed by free trade.

There are a number of strategies a firm can use to help it deal with the consequences of internationalisation, including offshoring and adding value.

☐ OFFSHORING

The increased liberalisation and deregulation of domestic markets around the world has led to firms looking more closely at offshoring as an option for dealing with global competition. Offshoring occurs whenever firms locate part of their business operations in other countries.

Firms have become increasingly more open to the idea of offshoring as they believe they may be able to gain significant cost advantages from doing so. These cost advantages might include lower transport costs, cheaper labour, cheaper raw materials and components, or favourable government policies with regard to corporation tax or environmental regulations.

Other firms, however, have been reluctant to offshore as they have concerns about the impact it could have on the quality of their goods or services. In addition, they may also be reluctant to offshore due to concerns about the impact it would have on their reputation in the domestic market.

If a company offshores some of its productive processes to another country then it can be classified as a multinational. A multinational enterprise (MNE) or a multinational corporation (MNC) is a firm that manages operations or has productive capacity in at least two countries. Well-known multinationals include companies like Nike, Cadbury Schweppes and Bombardier.

Multinationals have become increasingly important to the world economy. Some have incomes which are larger than the GDP of many of the countries in which they operate. Indeed, research shows that of the 100 largest economies in the world, 51 are corporations and only 49 are countries.

ACTIVITY 6.3

HSBC bank "to offshore more jobs"

Global bank HSBC says it expects to offshore more clerical jobs from Western countries to Asia in order to cut costs.

The world's second-largest bank already has 13,000 workers in call centres in India, China and the Philippines, and said yesterday it expects this number to rise to 25,000 in the next three years.

CEO Alan Jebson pointed out that the bank saved about £10,000 for every job it moved, and also stated that so far there had been no "significant adverse reaction" from customers.

(Adapted from BBC News website, 16 March 2005)

HSBC's statement was criticised by trade unions which see it as clear evidence of big businesses putting profits before the needs of staff and customers. The banking union UNIFI claims that over 4,000 jobs have been lost in the HSBC over the last few years as a result of offshoring. It also argues that UK consumers are becoming increasingly upset about having their queries routed to Asian call centres.

1. Explain what is meant by the term 'offshoring', and describe how it differs from outsourcing.
2. Explain three advantages HSBC might gain from offshoring jobs to Asia.
3. Explain some of the difficulties HSBC might experience as a result of offshoring in call centre operations.

☐ ADDING VALUE

Another option open to Northern Ireland firms when dealing with the consequences of globalisation is to focus on investing in the value-added dimension of their productive processes, and compete with foreign firms not on the basis of price but on the basis of quality, design and brand reputation.

For example, some UK textile firms which have been faced with increasing competition from low-cost producers in Asia have begun to specialise in the research, development and design functions of the productive process. They then license this intellectual property to foreign producers which manufacture and sell the products under the brand name of the UK firm.

Exchange rates

The increasing trend towards globalisation means that firms are more open to external factors which can affect their competitiveness in international markets. One such factor is the exchange rate.

The exchange rate is the price of one currency in terms of another. In other words, it is the rate at which one currency trades for another on the forex market. For example, £1 = $1.88 or £1 = €1.44.

The importance of the exchange rate in determining a firm's competitiveness should not be understated. Many UK businesses have failed as a result of unexpected changes in the exchange rate which led to their goods becoming uncompetitive in world markets.

©iStockphoto.com/molka

ACTIVITY 6.4

Currencies and exchange rates

1. Use the internet or the national press to find the currency used by the following countries:

UK	Republic of Ireland	France	US
Japan	China	India	

2. Using the internet, find the current value of sterling (£) against the following currencies.
   (a) Yen   £1 = ? yen
   (b) Dollar   £1 = ? dollars
   (c) Euro   £1 = ? euros
   (d) Yuan   £1 = ? yuan

3. Using the figures you have collected, calculate the export price, in each of the above countries, of a UK car which costs £22,000.

☐ CHANGES IN THE EXCHANGE RATE

The graphs below show how the value of sterling changed against the dollar and the euro between January and December 2006.

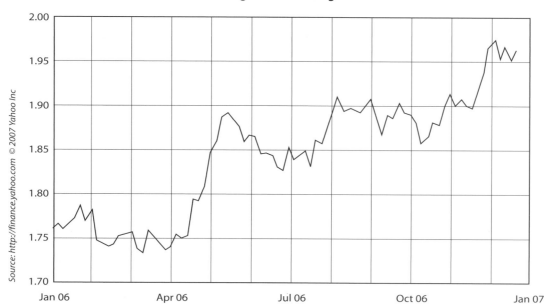

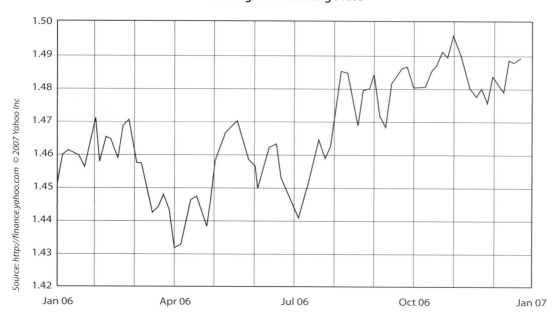

It is clear from looking at these graphs that the value of sterling fluctuates quite significantly against both the dollar and the euro.

These changes in the rate of exchange between countries can have a huge impact on export and import prices, and therefore will have an impact on the quantity of goods traded.

Depreciation

If one currency falls in value against another, it is described as a depreciation. For example, if £1 was equal to $1.88 and the pound depreciated, it would now be worth less in dollars, ie £1 = $1.20.

This depreciation of sterling would lead to UK exports becoming more competitive and imports into the UK becoming less competitive.

To understand why a depreciation of sterling would lead to UK exports becoming more competitive, consider a Northern Ireland based firm which produces goods for export to the US. If the sterling price of the good is £100, then under the initial exchange rate of £1 = $1.88 the dollar price of the good in the US would be $188 (£100 x $1.88).

Whenever sterling depreciates to £1 = $1.20, the dollar price of the good falls to $120 (£100 x $1.20). Therefore, a fall in the sterling exchange rate against the dollar leads to a fall in the dollar price of Northern Ireland exports.

Similarly, consider a good which is produced in the US and is imported into Northern Ireland. If the dollar price of the good is $200, then under the initial exchange rate the sterling price of the good would be £106.38 ($200 ÷ $1.88).

Whenever sterling depreciates to £1 = $1.20, the sterling price of the imported good increases to £166.67 ($200 ÷ $1.20). Therefore, a fall in the sterling exchange rate against the dollar leads to a rise in the sterling price of Northern Ireland imports from the US.

Chrysler garage, Belfast

Appreciation

If one currency rises in value against another, this is described as an appreciation. For example, if £1 was equal to $1.88 and the pound appreciated in value then it would now be worth more in dollars, ie £1 = $2. This appreciation of sterling would lead to UK exports becoming more expensive and therefore less competitive, and would make imports into the UK less expensive and therefore more competitive.

To understand why, consider again the Northern Ireland based firm which produces goods for export to the US. If the sterling price of the good is £100, then under the initial exchange rate of £1 = $1.88 the dollar price of the good in the US would be $188 (£100 x $1.88).

Whenever sterling appreciates to £1 = $2, the dollar price of the good increases to $200 (£100 x $2). Therefore, a rise in the sterling exchange rate against the dollar leads to an increase in the dollar price of Northern Ireland exports.

In the same way, consider again the good which is produced in the US and is imported into Northern Ireland. If the dollar price of the good is $200, then under the initial exchange rate the sterling price of the good would be £106.38 ($200 ÷ $1.88).

Whenever sterling appreciates to £1 = $2, the sterling price of the imported good falls to £100 ($200 ÷ $2). Therefore, an increase in the sterling exchange rate against the dollar leads to a fall in the sterling price of US products in Northern Ireland and therefore makes them more competitive.

To test your understanding of how exchange rate changes affect the price and therefore the competitiveness of exports and imports, consider the example in Activity 6.5 overleaf.

ACTIVITY 6.5

Changes in exchange rates

1. Use the table below to calculate the *export* price of a UK car under the different exchange rates.

Price of car (£)	Exchange rate	Price of car (€)
£22,000	£1 = €1.30	?
£22,000	£1 = €1.60	?
£22,000	£1 = €1.10	?

2. What happens to the export price of a car when the pound:
(a) appreciates
(b) depreciates

3. Use the table below to calculate the *import* price of a car under the different exchange rates.

Price of car (€)	Exchange rate	Price of car (£)
€22,000	£1 = €1.30	?
€22,000	£1 = €1.60	?
€22,000	£1 = €1.10	?

4. What happens to the import price of a car when the pound:
   (a) appreciates
   (b) depreciates

ACTIVITY 6.6

UK textiles in decline

The textiles and clothing industry was once one of Northern Ireland's largest manufacturing sectors, but the industry has been hit by one of the deepest slumps in its history. Between 2002 and 2007, production has collapsed by 30%, and employment in the sector has fallen by over 50%.

Some commentators argue that this collapse in textiles is an unavoidable consequence of natural changes in comparative advantage. They argue that Northern Ireland textile producers should be looking to increase investment and shift production towards higher quality and higher priced textiles. They claim that this type of output would have a more inelastic demand and would be less sensitive to the impact of exchange rate fluctuations.

1. Using a numerical example, explain how an increase in the exchange rate would cause the price of Northern Ireland exports to increase.
2. Explain why the introduction of the UK National Minimum Wage in 1998 would cause Northern Ireland textiles to become less competitive.
3. The last paragraph states that "Northern Ireland textile producers should be looking to increase investment and shift production towards higher quality and higher priced textiles." Explain the rationale behind this view.

Trading blocs

In an attempt to avoid the damaging effects of trade barriers, groups of countries will often join together to form a trading bloc. These blocs encourage trade between members and set up barriers to trade with non-members.

Examples of trading blocs include:

- The North American Free Trade Agreement (NAFTA)
- The Latin American Free Trade Association (LAFTA)
- The European Union (EU)

There are various different types of trading bloc, which vary according to the level of integration and cooperation between members. Some of the more common examples are considered below.

FREE TRADE AREA

In a free trade area members reduce or abolish restrictions on trade between each other, but retain individual barriers against non-members. The NATFA is an example of a free trade area. NAFTA's members are the US, Canada and Mexico. There are no restrictions on the movement of goods between these three countries, but each country is free to impose whatever barriers it chooses on goods from non-member countries.

CUSTOMS UNION

A customs union is similar to a free trade area in that barriers to trade between member countries are abolished. However, in a customs union a common (or identical) tariff is also applied by all members on goods imported from non-members. An example of a customs union is the South African Customs Union (SACU) which includes South Africa, Botswana, Namibia, Lesotho and Swaziland.

COMMON MARKET

In a common or single market other barriers to trade are abolished to allow the free movement of labour and capital as well as products and services. The European Single Market came into effect on 1 January 1993 and works on the basis of four freedoms – the free movement of goods, labour, services and capital throughout the EU.

ECONOMIC UNION

An economic union is the final stage of economic integration. It occurs when, in addition to creating common markets, member countries also seek to harmonise national economic policy. For full economic union to exist the member countries must operate under the same monetary and fiscal policy regime. The EU is an example of a trading bloc which is moving towards full economic union, with the introduction of a common currency and therefore a common monetary policy in 13 of the 27 member states.

The European Union

The first step on the road to what we know today as the EU was the formation of the European Coal and Steel Community (ECSC), in 1952 by France, Germany, Italy, Luxembourg, Belgium and the Netherlands.

In 1957 the same countries signed the Treaty of Rome and the European Economic Community (EEC) was formed. The Treaty of Rome established the EEC as a customs union. It stated that the six countries would over time withdraw all tariffs on trade in goods between the six members, but would impose a common external tariff on goods coming into the EEC from non-members.

The UK had decided not to join the EEC in 1958, feeling that it was a largely irrelevant organisation and preferring to maintain strong links with the US. It did, however, join the European Free Trade Association (EFTA) which, like the EEC, aimed to promote trade between members but did not impose common external tariffs.

By 1962 the UK government realised it had made a mistake and applied for entry to the EEC. Initially, its entry was blocked by the French, who felt that the UK was not committed to European integration. The UK reapplied ten years later and it joined in 1973, along with the Republic of Ireland and Denmark.

(Keystone/Staff/Getty Images)

The 1980s saw further enlargement of the EEC, with Greece, Spain and Portugal all joining. In 1985 the member countries signed the Single European Act. This act committed the countries to removing the many other non-tariff barriers to trade and to the formation of a genuine single market by 1993.

Delegates at the signing of the Treaty of Rome

As stated earlier, the European Single Market was based on four key freedoms – the free movement of goods, services, labour and capital throughout the whole of the EU. What this meant was that from 1993 companies could buy and sell goods and services without them being subject to trade barriers, workers could work in any member state and have their qualifications recognised, and businesses were free to operate in any member state.

In 1992 the 12 members signed another important treaty known as the Maastricht Treaty. This was a very wide-ranging treaty which covered areas other than trade. The Maastricht Treaty (also known as the Treaty of European Union) included provisions for a common security and defence policy and a common social policy. Significantly, it also included provisions for Economic and Monetary Union (EMU).

The signing of the Maastricht Treaty led to the renaming of the EEC – from that date it became known as the European Union (EU). This change in name was an attempt to reflect the fact that cooperation and integration was occurring in areas other than just the economy.

In 1995 the EU expanded again, with the inclusion of three new members – Austria, Finland and Sweden.

©iStockphoto.com/MistikaS

On 1 January 2002 euro notes and coins were introduced in the 12 participating states, and over the next few months their national currencies were phased out.

On 1 May 2004 the EU went through its biggest enlargement programme to date, with ten new members from Eastern Europe joining. On 1 January 2007 a further two Eastern European countries – Bulgaria and Romania – joined, bringing the current membership to 27.

Date	Country (Countries in bold are also members of Eurozone)	Total membership
25 March 1957	**Belgium, France, West Germany, Italy, Luxembourg, Netherlands** – founding members	6
1 January 1973	Denmark, **Ireland**, United Kingdom	9
1 January 1981	**Greece**	10
1 January 1986	**Portugal, Spain**	12
1 January 1995	**Austria, Finland,** Sweden	15
1 May 2004	Cyprus, Czech Republic, Estonia, Hungary, Latvia, Lithuania, Malta, Poland, Slovakia, **Slovenia**	25
1 January 2007	Bulgaria, Romania	27

☐ THE EURO

The euro (€) is the official currency of the 13 EU states which make up the **Eurozone.** It came into being as a real currency on 1 January 2002 when euro notes and coins were issued for the first time, but it had been a virtual currency for two years prior to this date.

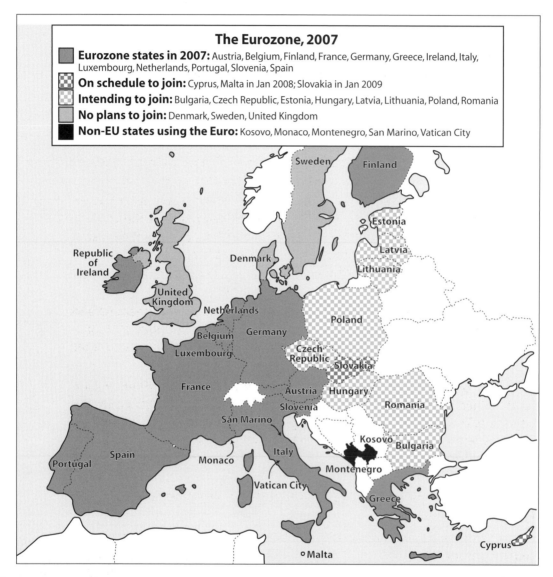

The Eurozone, 2007

- **Eurozone states in 2007:** Austria, Belgium, Finland, France, Germany, Greece, Ireland, Italy, Luxembourg, Netherlands, Portugal, Slovenia, Spain
- **On schedule to join:** Cyprus, Malta in Jan 2008; Slovakia in Jan 2009
- **Intending to join:** Bulgaria, Czech Republic, Estonia, Hungary, Latvia, Lithuania, Poland, Romania
- **No plans to join:** Denmark, Sweden, United Kingdom
- **Non-EU states using the Euro:** Kosovo, Monaco, Montenegro, San Marino, Vatican City

The euro cannot be described as the currency of the EU, since not all EU members have adopted it. Those countries which have recently joined the EU are obliged to join the euro within a certain time frame, since admission to the EU is dependant upon support for the single currency, but older members such as the UK are under no such obligation. The euro has also been adopted by some small European states which are not officially members of the EU, for example Vatican City, Monaco and Andorra.

In order to join the euro, countries must first meet certain conditions known as the convergence criteria. These convergence criteria are as follows:

- The country's inflation rate should be no more than 1.5% above the average of the three lowest members.
- Interest rates should be no more than 2% above the average of the three lowest members.

- The national currency must have been inside the Exchange Rate Mechanism (ERM) of the European Monetary System (EMS) for at least two years prior to entry to EMU.
- Regarding fiscal policy, the national budget should be no more than 3% of GDP and the accumulated national debt should not exceed 60% of GDP.

At present, the UK has opted out of the single currency as it believes that under the current economic climate the UK's interests would not be advanced through joining. However, the Labour government has committed itself to joining the euro whenever the economic conditions are right for the UK. Ultimately, the decision to join the euro will be taken by the UK electorate, since the government has promised to hold a referendum on the issue before making any decision.

THE IMPACT OF EU MEMBERSHIP ON THE NORTHERN IRELAND ECONOMY

The UK joined the EU in 1973 because it felt that being a member would lead to huge increases in trade between the UK and the EU, resulting in improved living standards for all UK citizens.

However, the potential benefits of EU membership on the Northern Ireland economy have been reduced by the fact that Northern Ireland is geographically on the periphery of the EU. This geographical isolation has made it more difficult for Northern Ireland firms to make the most of the opportunities created by the UK's membership of the EU. There has been a negative impact on manufacturing trade in particular, since Northern Ireland firms have higher-than-average transport costs.

In addition, as the only region of the UK with a land border with the Eurozone, Northern Ireland has been particularly affected by the introduction of the euro. The relative strength of sterling against the euro is having an adverse effect on the competitiveness of Northern Ireland firms relative to firms in the Republic of Ireland.

Nonetheless, membership of the EU has brought many benefits to the Northern Ireland economy. Since the UK joined the EU in 1973, up until 1993, Northern Ireland qualified for the highest level of EU funding. This is because it was classified as having "Objective One status" – in other words, its GDP was less than 75% of the EU average. This Objective One status meant that Northern Ireland qualified for funding from the EU to assist the economic and social development of the region.

This funding has had a significant impact on the Northern Ireland economy in terms of improving infrastructure and job opportunities.

Between 1989 and 1999 Northern Ireland received £1.75 billion from the EU Structural Funds programme. This money was used to:

- Implement the Common Agricultural Policy and assist farmers
- Develop the transport network and energy infrastructure
- Assist small businesses and tourism
- Boost training and education

Examples of projects undertaken with EU Structural Funds include:

- Waterfront Hall – £4 million
- Belfast–Dublin railway upgrade – £48 million
- Building the gas pipeline from Scotland to Northern Ireland and the electricity interconnector, both of which have resulted in lower energy prices for Northern Ireland consumers

Waterfront Hall, Belfast

Northern Ireland has also received over £400 million from the Peace Programme. This money has been spent mainly on community projects.

After 1999 Northern Ireland no longer qualified for Objective One funding, but it continued to receive a broadly similar level of funding. This was because the EU made Northern Ireland a special case and continued to fund it at the Objective One level in order to help create a more peaceful, prosperous and stable society.

There is little doubt, therefore, that Northern Ireland has benefited greatly from membership of the EU. The vast amounts of money invested in the Northern Ireland economy by the EU have had positive effects on economic growth and employment in the region. GDP in Northern Ireland now sits at 82% of the EU average (well above the threshold for Objective One funding) and unemployment rates are well below that of countries such as France, Italy, Spain and Sweden.

It is not just the funding which has benefited the Northern Ireland economy. Businesses here have been quick to take advantage of the opportunities offered to them through the single market and this too has had a positive effect on employment and growth.

The EU is not a 'done deal'. It has grown and changed dramatically since its inception in 1952 and it will continue to adapt and change as new treaties are signed and new countries join. Just what form the EU will take ten years from now and what part, if any, the UK will play in any future union is difficult to know. What we do know is that the EU will continue to have a massive influence on the economic performance of the UK and Northern Ireland economies.

REVISION QUESTIONS

1. Explain what is meant by the term 'international trade'.
2. Give three reasons why Northern Ireland firms would wish to trade internationally.
3. Give three advantages to the Northern Ireland economy of firms engaging in international trade.
4. Explain three arguments in favour of restricting international trade.
5. Explain what is meant by the term 'trade barrier'.
6. Explain three different types of trade barrier.
7. Define the term 'globalisation'.
8. Explain the term 'multinational enterprise', using an example to illustrate your answer.
9. Explain the impact an appreciation of sterling would have on the price of:
   (a) Northern Ireland exports
   (b) Imports into Northern Ireland
10. Explain the difference between a customs union and a common market.
11. Explain two benefits Northern Ireland firms gain as a result of UK membership of the EU.

CASE STUDY

645 jobs going at aerospace firm Bombardier
(Adapted from BBC News website, 24 and 25 October 2006, and other sources)

More than 600 jobs are going at the Belfast aerospace company Shorts, parent company Bombardier has said. The firm said yesterday that 645 jobs would go in its Northern Ireland plant and that all levels would be affected. The job losses will begin in January 2007.

Bombardier is Northern Ireland's largest manufacturing employer. The company had a turnover of £478.6 million and a reported net profit of £22.1 million in 2005.

Bombardier president Pierre Beaudoin justified the job cuts, stating they had to ensure "we achieve our goal of increased profitability and our success in the long term. This means making difficult but necessary decisions".

The company explained the need for job cuts by claiming that as a result of growing competition from low-cost economies, and the financial difficulties faced by US airlines in the wake of September 11th, there was lower demand in the worldwide market for its regional jets.

Bombardier has also said there is no connection between the growth of its operation in Mexico and the loss of the jobs in Belfast. About 1,200 new jobs are to be created in its Mexico plant at the same time as it is shedding a similar number of jobs in Northern Ireland and Canada. Bombardier said in a statement, "In relation to Bombardier's Mexico facility, there is absolutely no connection between the expansion in the Mexico plant and the announcement yesterday of the reduction of manpower levels in Belfast and Montreal."

Peter Robinson, DUP MP for East Belfast, said the job cuts would have a severe impact on the Northern Ireland economy. Bombardier employs about 5,300 of its total 26,900 workforce in Belfast. In terms of salaries and wages alone Bombardier provides £135 million per year into the local economy from its employees.

Sinn Féin's economic spokesperson Mitchel McLaughlin said the job losses highlighted the dangers of globalisation. He said "Sinn Féin has been arguing for some time that the structural weaknesses in the local economy will not be overcome through an overreliance on foreign direct investment."

Some local commentators have also questioned the decision of Bombardier to cut jobs so soon after securing almost £9 million in funding from Invest Northern Ireland last year.

Using the information above, answer the questions below.

1. Using the information in the second paragraph, calculate Bombardier's net profit ratio (net profit as a percentage of total revenue) for 2005.
2. Using demand and supply analysis, explain in detail the reasons for the job cuts as mentioned in the fourth paragraph.
3. Give two reasons why Mexico might be a more attractive place than Northern Ireland to build aeroplanes.

Mitchel McLaughlin stated that the job losses highlighted the dangers of globalisation.

4. Explain what is meant by the term 'globalisation'.
5. Explain three reasons why globalisation has increased in recent years.
6. One local commentator has claimed that "the continued strength of sterling has been a major factor in undermining the competitiveness of the Belfast plant". Evaluate the validity of this viewpoint.

COPYRIGHT INFORMATION

The following tradenames and trademarks are owned by their respective copyright holders:

Adidas, AOL, Apple, Ariel, Audi, Bank of Ireland, Bank of Scotland, BMW, The Body Shop, Bombardier, BP, British Sugar, BT, Bubblicious, C&C, Cadbury, Caterpillar, Clorets, Dell, Dentyne, eBay, EMI, ExxonMobil, FG Wilson, First Trust, George at Asda, Golden Wonder, Grove Services, Halifax, Harland and Wolff, HBOS, HP, HSBC, IBM, Interbew, Invest NI, Irish Salt Mining & Exploration Company, JD Sports, JJB Sports, John Lewis, Mars, Matalan, Maybin, MBG, McDonald's, Microsoft & Microsoft Windows, Montupet, Nestlé, New Look, Nike, Northern Bank, Northern Ireland Electricity, Peacocks, Persil, Pixar, PricewaterhouseCoopers, Primark, Quinn Group, Readymix, Reebok, Ryanair, Shell, Shorts, Sony, Tate & Lyle, Tayto, Tesco, Time Warner, Toni & Guy, Translink (Citybus, Northern Ireland Railways, Ulsterbus), Ulster Bank, Universal, Virgin Media, Warner, Wrigley, Yellow Pages

Colourpoint
Educational

Rewarding Learning

Colourpoint Educational has published another book in this series to address GCE Applied Business A2 Unit 7: Finance.

It covers all the relevant areas of the Specification, with examples, activities and revision questions included throughout to extend and reinforce learning.

ISBN: 978 1 904242 74 1
Price: £10.99
Author: Ian Bickerstaff

Contact Colourpoint Educational at:

Tel: **9182 0505**   Fax: **9182 1900**
Email: **sales@colourpoint.co.uk**
Web: **www.colourpoint.co.uk**

Colourpoint Books, Colourpoint House, Jubilee Business Park,
21 Jubilee Road, Newtownards, Co Down, BT23 4YH